OBSERVING AND DIAGNOSING AMERICA

OTOLORIN BELL, NMD

Observing and Diagnosing America

Copyright © 2021 by Otolorin Bell, NMD.

Paperback ISBN: 978-1-63812-146-6
Ebook ISBN: 978-1-63812-147-3

All rights reserved. No part in this book may be produced and transmitted in any form or by any means, electronic, or mechanical, including photocopying, recording, or by any information storage and retrieval system, without permission in writing from the copyright owner.

The views expressed in this work are solely those of the author and do not necessarily reflect the views of the publisher hereby disclaims any responsibility for them.

Published by Pen Culture Solutions 11/18/2021

Pen Culture Solutions
1-888-727-7204 (USA)
1-800-950-458 (Australia)
support@penculturesolutions.com

CONTENTS

Introduction vii
Chapter 1 The Plight of the New Immigrants and Their
           Vulnerabilities 1
Chapter 2 The Separation and Classification of Immigrants by
           the Justice Department, Office of Immigration, and
           Naturalization 6
Chapter 3 Psychology of Divide and Rule 9
Chapter 4 The Media, the Jobless Rate, and the Two Main Political
           Party Systems 11
Chapter 5 Denial of African Impact on the World Intellectual
           Plane.. 15
Chapter 6 The False Sense of Security of Some African
           Americans 18
Chapter 7 The Unequal Treatment of Black Immigrants under the
           Laws 23
Chapter 8 American Fronts on Knowledge and Intelligence 27
Chapter 9 Religious Persuasions in America 29
Chapter 10 American Attractions to Peddled Products 34
Chapter 11 On the Problem of Stable Family 37
Chapter 12 Recognizing the Difference of the Genders 43
Chapter 13 On the Population Makeup of the USA 48
Chapter 14 The Choice of Leadership in America 54
Chapter 15 Bring Them Down! 59
Chapter 16 The "Sins" of Bill Clinton 62
Chapter 17 Everyone Is Enjoying the Benefits of Clinton's
           Presidency.. 66
Chapter 18 The Fallibility of the American Power......................... 69

Chapter 19 The Parental Responsibility and Child Upbringing......76
Chapter 20 The Media as Instrument of Confusion........................79
Chapter 21 On Education..81
Chapter 22 Common Pattern of Resistance to Progressive
            Initiatives..85
Chapter 23 Ethnic Politics in the United States........................... 90
Chapter 24 Final Diagnosis 96
Bibliography 101

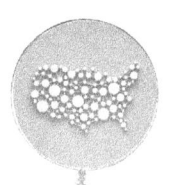

INTRODUCTION

This book is an attempt to focus attention of Americans to the problem they pose for themselves and other immigrants in their midst. Also, the book highlights the alienation usually felt by naturalized citizens of the United States.

Naturalized citizens and legal immigrants should be made to feel welcome both naturally and psychologically. Besides, early immigrants who had emigrated here from other parts of the world built the country. They just happened to be Europeans. It also highlights cycle of vicious behaviors on innocent population.

No one is qualified to question anyone's background. And no one is qualified enough to question the loyalty of another citizen just because they arrived here earlier. It is the contribution to progress and advancement of the nation, which should be the yardstick of love and loyalty. So also should payment of taxes and improvement and participation in civic duties. Overt pressure of questioning other citizens' accents and fluency in the English language is a sore note of discord for all races inhabiting this free land. Unfortunately, this and other attitudes drove the early settlers or immigrants to the near annihilation of the original dwellers––the Cherokee and other American Indians. Racist attitudes that were the bases of the founding of this modern American nation must be discarded.

Until all immigrants come to grip with the situation at hand and start treating one another with respect, and this coupled with the recognition of Native Americans rights and aspirations, the fabrics holding the nation together would sooner break apart at the seam.

CHAPTER 1

The Plight of the New Immigrants and Their Vulnerabilities

It all started with this immigrant maiden flight to New York City's JFK Airport from Ikeja Airport of my native city of birth, Lagos, Nigeria. Proud and happy but fearful of the uncertainties yet to come, I was scared of the dangers lurking in the corners of the intended nation called the USA. But I was determined to experience for myself as my friends who had made this journey before me wrote in their letters. I wanted to achieve a college education and graduate and return to contribute to the development of the native land.

After all, everyone who had been my closest friends from high school had journeyed here and even those who graduated from high school after I did had proudly taken up college education in the USA and had had something great to discuss of the experience. If America was this accommodating, why then did I have these mixed feelings on my flight? Once I had these gut feelings about anything, I know I was in for a bumpy experience, but I didn't know what to expect. Could I had been so weak in resolve that I was overwhelmed with emotions inexplicable even to myself? The fear of the unknown seems to be so much that I became numbed in my thoughts. To turn back was unthinkable even though part of me would. How would I face anyone back home when I was the one who gave words of courage to the despaired? I was Mr. Sociable and Mr. Tolerance, and Mr. Courage all rolled in one as judged and revered and secretly admired or envied by my peers and colleagues. If anyone was familiar with the odds I overcame in my young life despite being born to a well-to-do Nigerian family of nobility by any standard of the time and even of the contemporary time, he or she would not be surprised by my mature outlook on things.

I was hampered by the intricacies and paradoxes of the culture and its fortitude. A neutral observer would understand the handicap in totality. But that hurdle of my life would be a subject for an autobiography at some other time.

It began with the purchase I made at the Ikeja Airport in Nigeria, now Murtala Mohammed's International Airport. I bought an American *Newsweek* magazine for the last week of March 1972 at the airport. It was labeled the foreign edition. I used to subscribe to the *TIME* magazine (another American weekly news magazine). This was an attempt to get familiar with events going on in that awesome continent country just like a whole generation of my peers with such fascination with the USA and the people who inhabited the landscape. It bordered on brainwashing the wonderful stories of benevolence and godliness of America as a nation. Even the title on her currency denominations could not have said it better. The Voice of America never missed an opportunity to tell the poor third-world nation, in fact the rest of the world, how every minute of the day a millionaire was born. What that meant we would never know, but what followed this maiden flight of mine was to be a lesson of a lifetime.

It proved to me the ultimate loss of innocence of my life. Out of curiosity, I purchased another *Newsweek* magazine of the same period as the one purchased in Lagos, Nigeria. Only this time, this edition at JFK Airport did not have foreign edition label. Comparing the contents of the two magazines of the same period, I found too many discrepancies. Some stories, for instance, that were negative––coverage of members of the African-American community, for example––were given too much prominence in the foreign edition while scanty references were made to the same story for domestic consumption. This was a first sign of discomfort and I started to brace myself for more shocks. I was later to learn the arm-length friendliness of the Caucasian or "white" Americans. I also noticed the confused relationship of the

African-Americans with the Africans from the continent. In most countries of the world, the presence of a foreign individual if noticed, out of politeness, is not usually made obvious, but not in America (USA). Because of infantile developmental process which most of the people seem to have gone through, and because of the need to show or convince themselves that they could detect difference of accents in individuals, the foreign individual is immediately made aware of his or her foreignness. Imbeciles with little or nothing in their heads would approach the foreigner with no greeting or any form of diplomatic acquaintance or exchange with the question "Where are you from?" What a rude approach! The cultured foreigner out of politeness either would quietly ignore the rude intrusion. But the mannerless one from the USA would continue his or her question with as fake a smile as his/her ignorance would take her only to meet with a sharp rebuff. What would follow would be a labeling of the foreigner as a hostile one.

Because no American likes to accept any blame, it is difficult for an American to act collegiately unless their bread and butter is on the line. A foreigner who is too reasonable or polite is quickly labeled as timid or is in want of favor from the indigenous citizen and therefore treated with suspicion at best or hostility at worst.

Such is the state of confusion that a new immigrant or would-be immigrant is confronted with when he or she lands in the USA. All the concocted image of the American through the movies, radio, or American newspapers run diametrically opposed to the real picture once you're on the ground. Worse still, the average American, black or white in general, paint an unrealistic picture of this country bordering on heaven on earth. Very few citizens of the United States of America ever attempt to set the record straight and lay bare for a foreigner what to expect. What is worse is that the immigrant, after a few years in the United States, return to his previous country to paint a lofty picture of the new country and soon join the charade like other individuals suffering from Americanism. This whole painting of course is often for the foreigner in a foreign country or a short-time-staying visitor to the United States with no intention of staying. However, once the visitor intends to stay and declared that intention, the rule of the relationship changes. From there on, it's dog-eat-dog and the definition of turf of operation.

The new immigrant who had looked upon the country with awe and all the respect of the world based on the carefully constructed, brainwashing image painted for him/her came to face the reality of what America is. An otherwise pleasant, gullible person came to the USA to face a hostile community with no one to turn to in this new adopted nation. No hands of warmth were ever extended to this newcomer who no matter his/her ability to speak the language of the majority howbeit with an accent. The impact would only be cushioned if the newcomer landed in an area where many of these ethnic homeland foreigners inhabit. This way he may be able to get an education on how to deal with these hostile hosts who present themselves as hospitable beings in foreign lands. On the other hand, depending on the disposition and awareness of the new would-be immigrant, his views may be at variance with his former compatriots who may have painted far too hopeless a picture for him to grapple with and may therefore set in motion far worse a reaction in him more than was intended. This is the classic example of the culture shock often spoken about but poorly understood in terms of the USA, third-world people interactions. Part of the reason for the new immigrant who may have joined in the premature praise of America or Americans is his difficulty of differentiating the system from the people and also the laws and their implementation and all the biases built into the executions. Other reasons may be of a case of personal frame of references. The immigrant joining a chorus of praise for America may do so because of fear of being labeled a failure and a sour grape in the midst of other "successful" immigrants who probably are European and are apolitical and just plain lucky. Some of the African immigrants have had modest successes too, especially professionally except that very few of them ever get to practice what they went to school or college for. But nonetheless, they can be thankful that they are able to eat and look well within the premise of physical appearance. Other than survival, nothing else!

But wherever and whenever the immigrant African is elevated and the worth of his/her contributions finally required, the pressure to succeed and remain on the only job, which may be the only one they would ever have that would pay them equally for their professional accomplishment, becomes intense and almost discomforting. Many would finally develop high blood pressure and suffer from stroke and heart ailment, which eventually would prove more deadly before they run back to their country of origin if they are smart enough before it is too late. For if they stay too long and remain trapped with the illusion of success, their remembrance of what they were in their home country would have been forgotten and erased in memory.

In all, the coming to the USA by the new immigrant gives a new meaning to the classic survival of the fittest of the evolution theory. But with determination, a lot of luck, and ultimate support from God, the innocent immigrant may survive his/her isolation or become sucked in by various former immigrants or U.S. con artist of all shades.

CHAPTER 2

The Separation and Classification of Immigrants by the Justice Department, Office of Immigration, and Naturalization

The whole exercise of separation and classification of immigrants according to their race already got the stamp of racism embedded in the policy of a nation, which prides herself on evenhandedness. No, there was never an evenhandedness in the treatment of people who immigrated into the United States of America. The classification already gave unfair advantage to the holders of the British and Dutch passports. These immigrants would not need a visa for their first ninety days in the United States. In other words, citizens of these nations could enter the United States without the requirement of an entry visa. Other nationals of European nations get their visa on demand once it was declared that they are non-Communists. The speed of approval of their visa for immigrant status for most of the Western European nationals is phenomenal. From then on, the preferential treatment knows no bound once in the country. They can move from the Northeast to the Northwest and the Southeast to the Southwest and into the Midwest cracker country and deep South redneck with no hindrance while they create their own niche without question irrespective of their educational background. The Western Europeans are first among equals in the eye of the United States' immigration and naturalization office.

Next is the political consideration for speedy processing of the East European refugees fleeing Communist enclaves when they exited. The Russian non-Communists also follow this group of East Europeans. But because of the enormous influence the Jewish ethnic group wields over the United States's Justice and the State Departments, the papers of members of this ethnic group receive special, speedy treatment for imagined or real sense of persecution from any of their previous host countries. The special treatment I believe stem from the enormous way members of the Jewish group has over vital areas of the United States's lifeline and also from the sense of guilt for the complicity that had been displayed by the European and the Caucasian Americans over the treatment of the Jews in Hitler's Germany. The Jews will never let the Americans forget it as if they (the Americans) actually caused the pogrom in Germany during the reign of the Third Reich.

The Arabs of the Middle East and the Muslims of Persia are lumped with the Turks in treatment. Their religious belief in Islam makes the United States's policymakers uneasy. That religion makes this group very mercurial and difficult to dominate as their philosophy on life is divergent from the Judeo-Christian view of life. Some Arabs or Persians who profess Christianity have easier treatments only to realize that that is where the preferential treatment ends. The classification at the bottom of the skin ladder persists. Their classification is only slightly better rated than the Asian and Indians and the Africans and people of the African descent.

Next to the Middle Eastern immigrants are the Asians led by the Japanese and the Chinese. These groups are the reluctant immigrants, culturally and philosophically different from the rest of the world. The Indians also fit into the mold. Their religious beliefs are as varied as the clothes of the rest of the world. At best, they're treated warily and with some caution and respect by the American populace once they pass through the immigration scrutiny. After all, most learned Americans have read about Confucius's philosophy of the dynasties of the Chinese and the miracle of the civilizations existing thousands of years before the American nation was born or built or founded.

Selective treatments of the people of the South Americans or the Latinos only equal the treatments meted to the Africans by the immigration officers. It is not the clerk's fault the policy of selective and quota determination for eligibility has been handed down from the top. And being only clerks, they bring into play their own subjective ill-advised sentiments into the approval and rejection process.

The assault on the innocent African immigrant who perhaps shares more in common with the American philosophical setting than even the Western Europeans has been in motion even before he sets his foot on the American soil. He has been classified and assigned measured treatment as "befits" his/her race along with the Americans who share part of his genetic ancestry. This is the bottom of the pack. The African is then blamed, insulted, and manhandled should he react to this lesser-than-human treatment.

The justification often is that he was never treated better in his home country from where he journeyed to the United States of America. This is the same justification used in the slave trade and the treatment of the slaves from the African continent. A total fallacy! If the purveyor of these lies are courageous and enlightened enough to reveal the truth, they would let it be known that despite poverty in the continent, the Africans even to date are still able to dream freely of one day holding the high office of his mother- and fatherland unlike his or her African American cousins who have been relegated and continues to be browbeaten because of their racial inheritance.

Even in these modern times, racial consideration is used largely in the election into the legislative and executive branches of both state and federal governments and not the content of the character and intellect of the individuals occupying the offices. Retaliation and necessity to uplift and negate the African characterization weighs more in the election of the African Americans elected to public offices. This is the same racial necessity that the Caucasians adopted. How else could anyone explain the election and reelections of characters such as Jesse Helms of North Carolina and Strom Thurmond of South Carolina and their likes into the United States Senate? No one ever threatened their lives because of the racial positions they advanced. In fact, they received all the necessary accolades of respect whenever applicable.

CHAPTER 3

Psychology of Divide and Rule

Here in the United States, the African and his descendant cousins, brothers, and sisters have been relegated and classified derogatorily. What is worse, the Caucasian has brainwashed the Mongolians of Asian descent to believe the false premise of the classification that they have superior intellect than the African even when they know the opposite is true in their hearts and in their practical contacts with the African and his descendent cousins born in the United States of America and the Caribbean and South America. Every intellectual pursuit and puzzles both in sports and other spheres ever created or adopted or stolen by the Caucasian, the African and his descendants have been able to master it and even created its own diversity of such creations presented to him and which the Caucasian and Asian appendage often find difficult to understand let alone master.

With his success, and loyalty to the USA beyond question, the African American descendants never got the same appreciation or rewarded in the same measure as their Caucasian counterparts. Exceptions in this category are not the rule. To hold any position, the African and his cousins must prove to the Caucasian population that he or she is willing to be their stooge even against their kin and kits when they don't merit such treatment. He or she must also demonstrate some form of hostility against the Africans from the continent to the extent of denying kinship and supplanting it with American Indian ancestry.

Worse still, the Africans of Egypt, Morocco, Tunisia, and Libya are expected to deny their Africanism once they reach the United States of America or Western Europe, including Britain, for that matter. After all, the classification by Caucasians has separated them from their African brothers and sisters of the sub-Saharan desert.

No Caucasian has ever been required by any tacit anecdote to show the same behavior to the European immigrants no matter their accents, which by the way are considered by the American as "beautiful" spoken English even if they cannot speak the language.

Rapprochement of the African Americans with the African immigrants was only achieved when the former never got rewarded by the system or treated worse sometimes in an attempt by the Caucasian at the apex of power of the establishment to show his toughness on the black employee and convince his other Caucasian friend that he is not soft on the weak.

The whole behavior pattern reveals the incompetence and the unfairness of the Caucasian at any of the competitive tasks. It also shows the frailness of the ego and his inability to accept his incompetence with good attitude. The inferiority of the Caucasians to the people of African ancestry is further magnified by the obstacles they erect on the road of the Africans and her descendants in order to prevent the participation of the same at the task, which is intended to prove the ability of the individuals. And when such barriers are broken, the sneering begins, claiming genetic predetermined advantage at such tasks rather than face their own incompetence. I call this behavior not racism but unfair trade practices, which could be so labeled for such incompetent practices rather than allude to the superiority of one race over the other. Of course, we all know the truth with survival instincts in this unfair world given the built-in insecurities of the Caucasian race.

CHAPTER 4

The Media, the Jobless Rate, and the Two Main Political Party Systems

Many of the immigrants could never understand the reading and the computation of the U.S. jobless rate. The jobless rate actually reflects the number of the eligible U.S. workers receiving unemployment insurance pay from the labor department. Often, it only reflects mostly the Caucasian workers. The unemployment rate records the number of Caucasians unemployed and receiving unemployment insurance pay, discounting the tenth of the population or mostly blacks and other minorities. Those numbers do not account for the qualified but unemployed minorities due to their projection of confidence and take-charge readiness, not especially valued by the working class born in the USA with Caucasian middle management mentality. Many of them, having had their egos bruised several times, never bothered to look for a job anymore and never sought unemployment insurance pay.

By now most immigrants are able to identify the two prominent political parties of the USA. They are, for the record, the Democratic Party and the Republican Party. American historians have told us the Democratic Party was initially modeled after the Whig Party (Conservative Party) of Britain, and the Republican Party was for the poor people. But today, an interested observer would have a hard time deciding from their party labels which party is actually for the poor. The truth of the matter is that for every member of the Congress but a few, the vote goes to the highest bidder. While the Republican Party essentially has all but abandoned campaigning in the black districts, the Democrats are squirmy about it. But the Democrats still have room for redemption because of the freedom and latitude of the individual members. Unlike the Republican rank and file, which is gagged and bound over, the Democrats still show flashes of conscience in discharging their duties.

The appeal to the "white" Americans by the Republican Party leadership as their guardian against the "traitor" white Democrats from plundering the privilege runs hollow. The real people being safeguarded by the Republicans are the rich Anglo-Saxon Americans while the rough-and- tumble blue collar Caucasians are used as pawns and with condescending winks of the eye in the racial divide. This divide they (Republicans) continue to widen further, sending the country back to the dark ages of ignorance.

It used to be the issue of welfare checks to the needy that was used to whip up support against the African Americans living in the project houses in cities across the United States. Yet statistics of the welfare recipients show that nonblack or Caucasian recipients are about 80 percent. But this fact is deliberately lost on those making a point of the campaign of calumny. The Democrats were beaten on the head day by day by these hapless Republicans. These Democrats, devoid of how to respond to the Republicans, ran for cover until Bill Clinton came to power!

It was Bill Clinton who pulled the issue off the table of Republicans. It was Bill Clinton who found the way to restore the dignity to a dispossessed people who could not survive this dog-eat- dog world of capitalism. The civil right activists had no alternative. Neither did they offer one against the loss of welfare support for the recipients. The present clamor for social security insolvency by the Republican members of Congress is to deny the handful of nonwhite recipients if we look hard into their hearts, which they camouflage with "fiscal integrity" or "responsibility."

Now that the volunteer army through various financial promises seem to be drawing a lot of nonwhite citizens of able bodies, the Republican-minded whites in uniform will soon find ways to orchestrate dishonorable discharges of the majority of the nonwhite volunteer, thereby depriving them of the ability to enjoy the carrot put forward for their enlistment both in cash and promise of education after discharge if they survive the periods of their enlistment without being killed in a foreign war.

Whenever a Democrat panders to the Republican agenda and becomes wishy-washy to his constituents of nonwhite and some liberal Caucasians, the Democrat loses by tuning off the nonwhite electorates. These electorates sit the election out, leaving the fate of the Democrat in office in the hands of white or Caucasian electorate who invariably would bolt to the Republican line. It has happened in federal elections as well as local elections. This was what happened when President Jimmy Carter lost to challenger Ronald Reagan. But it was explained in terms of higher inflation and the lower self-esteem of the nation. It happened also when George Bush came from behind to trounce Michael Dukakis who despite his early lead in the polls forgot his core constituents, never really realizing that they mattered.

Some of the Democratic Party pundits, including African Americans, even deceive their candidates by telling them that blacks don't vote. What should have been explained was the blacks would not vote for a candidate they cannot truly trust would care for their needs or champion the cause of their lives.

The truth of the blurring of the differences of the two major political parties is rooted in the brainwashed frail egos of personal frame of reference in racism. Most white Democrats, mindful of their race and being protective of the unfair privileged advantage conferred on them as a result, are unwilling to tamper with the Republican position on the code of preservation of the species. In fact, for spite, Republicans often would ask the Democrats to embrace openly the well-documented notion of black equality with whites, which the Democrats would fail.

Now, the Republicans are trying to be careful or deceitful in their utterances since they discovered that an open-ended gaffe in their pronouncement may fire the blood of the African Americans and other minorities into going to the voting booth irrespective of the artificial barriers to vote for their opponents. They now talk in codes hoping for their white audience to catch on. But for the other minorities of the Hispanic and Asian descents too slow to realize that they are still classified below the "almighty" white race, most of the methods used for the "divide and rule" are already understood by the African American electorates.

It is equally difficult for the black candidates to express themselves on behalf of poor constituents without being labeled as radicals at best. Thank God for the collapse of the communist Soviet Russia. No one gets labeled anymore as communists. Until the media and the political leaders realize that equal treatment of citizens is what would strengthen the fabric of unity of the nation, all talks of a United States of America waxing stronger would be an illusion.

CHAPTER 5

Denial of African Impact on the World Intellectual Plane

The deliberate policy to undereducate Americans borrowed its leaf page from the Hollywood filmmaking culture long before the African American came on the scene. Even here, the immediate attention of these new entrants is to bring to the spotlight the lives lived by African Americans in the United States. This effort draws attention to the history of black people, their anguish, and pattern of denials by Caucasian compatriots from sharing the goods of this country instead of the crumbs. The African American movies try as much as possible to have the point that the people of African ancestry are human too and capable of feeling and hurt just like the Caucasians even if the melanin pigment of their skin prevents them from turning pink or white in times of emotional upheavals.

But the relegation of the Africans and their contribution to modern development has been allowed to go on for too long. Most of the narrow thinkers of Eurocentric extractions had been given free rein on the intellectual plane for too long. Many of these shallow writers have been allowed to deny their plagiarism of African philosophical observations while ascribing such to Europeans mostly of the Greek ancestry. At best, African philosophy were reduced to one-liner adages or statements. The American students were not allowed to learn of the various empires of Mali, Ghana, Songhai on West Africa. None of the American students in elementary or high schools was given the opportunity of knowing the importance of Timbuktu as the learning center where Pythagoras who was a great Greek mathematician became a student when he reached the city after initially accepting the job of a professor. Pythagoras found the mathematical knowledge of the students at the ancient learning center in West Africa more advanced than his own knowledge of algebra and geometry. This was the same center that the brightest of the Egyptian royalties have learned and studied philosophy several years before. Archeologists unearthed the architectural construction and planning of that ancient civilization reduced to rubbles by the barbarians from Rome and Greece after the news brought by the Greek philosophers of an advanced peaceful democracy in Africa.

Neither was it an accident as the playwright William Shakespeare wrote of the Moor in Othello. Alas, the poor European and American young people are denied the true knowledge of history because of the personal frame of reference of a few narrow-minded individuals who call themselves leaders of the world. The poor Caucasians were denied of the knowledge of the ignoble role played in Africa by the Europeans. The pillage and destruction caused on the African continent was treated as a mere footnote of history. This was the prelude to slave trade after the murder and genocide of the brightest on the continent, especially in West Africa. This assertion of the culpability of the American Caucasian (who emigrated from Europe) is borne out in their outlawing of the teaching or of any slave learning to read or write the English language. The Africans' previous learning method had been in their own language just as the Greeks or the Egyptians had learned in their own respective languages. From then on, the white Americans of all shades, especially the so-called conservatives, never really admit comparison or better ability from equal starting premise (which they never want to grant) for the children of all races. Instead, they want to rely on the false ego-boosting assessment of a biased Caucasian assessor.

No one has ever alluded to the stealing of the dialogue existing within the court of the Alafin, the king of the ancient Oyo Empire of West Africa. This system was copied by the ancient Greeks and consequently given credit for the birth of democracy. Neither would the propagandists give credence to the order of government created by the various empires before the advent of the European assault on the people of Africa.

Soon the world of medicine will turn to African herbal or homeopathic medicine (which has been ignored for hundreds of years) in solving some of the yet-intractable diseases afflicting mankind. For many years now, the Chinese medicine (herbal) has been touted and the philosophy extolled. So also has been the European herbal wonders, which employs a lot of the herbs from South American jungles (rainforest) and Africa's.

No one would attest to the closure of West African Textile industries and shutdown of liquor distillation by the Europeans who colonized West African Nations as they declared the industries illegal.

CHAPTER 6

The False Sense of Security of Some African Americans

You have never known a few people with the desire to break with their past so bad. You could say these individuals are running from their shadows. It is one thing to want to prove your Americanism. It is another to want to present yourself as having no origin and no sense of history. Even the Caucasian for whose love some of the African Americans described above are competing still make allusion to their European ancestry. Unfortunately, for these upstarts, the African genetic inheritance is so dominant that you cannot obliterate its phenotypical picture even in an albino.

A break with the African inheritance, because of a feeble financial success, actually depicts the picture of a coward not worthy of being born, let alone living. Little do these individuals know that they are living the scripts already written for them and prescribed for them to act—return to the slavery when the African slave was beaten silly to forget who he was, free born, of African nobility, and forced to accept the name of his owner like a collar around their necks like dogs.

Some of them had made more money in entertainment industry, some in in sports, and some still in the lofty professions of medicine, law, or finance. Worse still, some have called themselves religious ministers with no courage of moral conviction to stand for who they are. Instead, many of the African American clergy would preach to their flock as if they have no connection with any ancestry except the one they found on the soil of the United States of America. But for Malcolm X and a few lesser-known African Americans and Paul Robeson before Malcolm X, all would have been lost in tandem. It was an attempt by these African American rejectionists to walk the plank of the conservative labels affixed to them––another name was "Uncle Tom" who had more courage, by the way.

Many of these "conservative" African Americans have done or committed more havoc to themselves and their kin than the Caucasian Americans have done to the entire race of the African people. To show mettle, they often put down their youths (Africans Americans) without showing what they can do to uplift the community positively. If they have the position in which they could employ the qualified African American youth, they would not, often pointing to the negative reasons for not hiring these youths or applicants from their race. Instead, they have to be the lone African American in an establishment surrounding themselves with Caucasians. No one is saying that the Caucasians should not be hired for the job they're qualified for. But what we observe often is that the "conservative" African American often goes out of his way to deny his own kind of the job. They often could do better than the Caucasian hired in the first place.

The scenario is even worse for an African immigrant. Most often, the hostility could be read on the faces or body languages of these Uncle Toms. If they head the admission committee of institutions of higher learning, often the African immigrants are quickly denied admission along with the financial support necessary for such students to be able to pursue a successful academic career. Often, you find that a reprieve is often received from a Caucasian American for such African immigrant.

Such is the position an African immigrant is placed, making it difficult for him to close ranks with his cousins in the United States unless he is well schooled to treat such incidences an isolation rather than the rule. You just have to rise above this pet111ness and ignorance and deal with the source of the pettiness and ignorance.

This ignorance of the African American "conservative" had been fueled by the media and the image of the African implanted in the head and psyche of the homeboys and home girls. So one could understand the surprise and confusion experienced by the people when the behavior of some Africans they come in contact with does not fit the scripts. The ignorance is not limited to the African Americans. The Caucasians too have been undeserved by the media trying to promote their (Caucasians) dominance. Ignorance, like knowledge, cannot be disguised for too long before the identity of the holder is unmasked. Until these Uncle Toms are finally pushed down from their illusionary lofty heights or the home boys and home girls dealt with ruthlessly (using the law enforcement agencies) with denial of their basic human rights, then it will dawn on them that they were no better than their cousins from the African continent. Yet some, still shameless and lacking in personal integrity, would not observe the writing on the wall. Perhaps it's not integrity but lack of basic intelligence.

As if all the preceding nuances are not enough, the African immigrant would have to endure the stupid statement, "I was born here." What that is meant to convey to the immigrant who probably had older children born on the soil of the USA beats me. Perhaps noticing that the immigrant is still having remnants of a foreign accent is an indication of ignorance of what is happening in America. Or it is a protection of a nonexistent right of turf. Whatever is the underlying reason, whether proclaimed or kept inside the proclaimer of a birth right on the U.S. soil, the stupidity could not be more glaring.

Just as there are immigrants from other nations in the USA, so are thousands of U.S. citizens in all parts of the world carrying out their businesses in those foreign lands and bringing home the spoils from those capitals to make it a little easier for the son of the soil of the USA.

No wonder that some homeboys and home girls feel they could run roughshod against their brothers and sisters from across the Atlantic Ocean. They have or had this erroneous notion that they could commit varying degrees of crimes, which they would never dream of committing against any Caucasian, and get away with it. Sadly, the fools who pretend to be their teachers and role models are rearing damaged futures on the streets of America.

Many of the oppressed immigrants of Asian, Arabic, Jewish, and yes, African heritage have had their children opting for the plastic surgeon's knife to erase any semblance of their physical resemblance to their parents. This should not come as a shock. It is rather a result of the not-too- subtle pressure exerted on these children by the Caucasian society, which tend to want to accept what looks Caucasian and rejection of what does not. It is arguable that these children probably went too far because of their individual lack of self-esteem and pride in their races and uniqueness of their physical appearances. However, one must remember that while the Caucasian born in the USA wants to laugh readily at other cultures and physical appearances, he or she has zero tolerance for any non-Caucasian immigrant who would poke the same fun at the race. Such behavior secretly and overtly through official collective high handedness is treated as insubordination.

Although it is no longer the focus of the civil rights leadership––but it should––the agenda of the right-wing Caucasian born in the United States is to keep the family structure of the minority fragmented, disoriented, and distorted. Several black entertainers of the minority cloth are employed and encouraged through the boosting of their careers to trash the race on camera without provocation. Some even get delight in pulling down the heroes of the civil rights movement into disrepute. Many make jokes of the plight these heroes went through, even ridicule the movement if only to get a laugh from a hapless audience. The quiet leaders of the civil rights are also guilty of keeping the family issues in the backburner because of donations from the white establishments. The balance just needs to be maintained. Instead, the fight was shelved so as to make a disinterested party happy.

The Hispanic family structure is getting by and escaping the machination often suffered by the African American family because it has never lost the language advantage as the slave immigrants. They too have to undergo the mental agony of knowing where they belong. On one hand, they are resented by the blacks for coming to America just to enjoy what they (African Americans) suffered to attain. On the other, they are being subordinated by the Caucasians because of their refusal to take up and embrace the Caucasian lingua franca (English) and lifestyles. Therefore, the uneasy alliance, because of their number, would have to be formed with black Americans with continuous tussle for leadership. Once there is this muddle, the wall of cooperation is cracked, allowing the opportunistic interest to wade in. Unfortunately, the Native Americans are still hurting to be able to make their special impact felt on the land taken from them by force and connivance. Years of alcohol abuse and deep hurt have kept the community from focusing on the big prize, coupled with historical intertribal fight and bickering for supremacy.

The unity of these minority groups would put them on even keel with the dominant Caucasian group with regard to getting the chance to contribute to the betterment of the USA in the most humane manner. There is enough of the national cake to go around if only all groups would uphold and recognize this nation as everyone's responsibility to get to the point of perfection or near it. Thank God almighty Oprah Winfrey bounced back on top; Bill Cosby recovered from the tragic loss of his only son; Michael Jordan, he too recovered from the sudden loss of his dad. Vernon Jordan is still alive and breathing. Isaac Hayes is here. So are Jim Brown and James Brown, and the list goes on. Never should anyone forget that this is America, which resisted the education of the Negro slaves, the integration of the Negro into the mainstream. This is America which has and still is sponsoring state terrorism against heroes of the third-world nations. We are going to be understanding but not forgetting the heroes of years back, such as W. E. B. Dubois, Kwame Nkrumah, Ahmed Sekou Toure, Patrice Lumumba, Gamaliel Abdel Nasser. We will always remember the sacrifices of Martin Luther King, Jr., Malcolm Shabbaz X, Medgar Evers, and a host of the courageous lot in different fields of endeavor.

Although they make us laugh, the comedians among us touch and strike a chord of reaction from us even when they are not responsible for the scripts they are handed. The actors and scholars have also paid their dues even by risking ridicule from their own folks to break the color barrier. Every one of these people will tell you of the burden they had to bear. Again, we remember Paul Robeson, Sidney Poitier, Joe Louis, Jackie Robinson, Louis Armstrong, and the list goes on. No one should misrepresent this observation as a critique of any ethnic group. The world is small now and all embracing. The attention must be equivocal and balanced unless there is some chromosomal aberration, which has now taken place in human genome, causing a mutated reproduction of abnormality irreversible enough to dash the hope of mankind for redemption all over the world.

CHAPTER 7

The Unequal Treatment of Black Immigrants under the Laws

Most immigrants would want to believe that they have finally arrived at the last stop where justice would be impartial and administered evenly. But often, they found that depending on which country they emigrated from, they have several strikes against them. One of the biggest strikes is their accent in spoken English, if they can speak it at all. This difference in speaking pattern often invite harsher treatment from law enforcement officers who often believe they could get away with murder with these immigrants. Because they don't speak with the accent of the land, the law officers and officers of the court often have no patience to hear them out if they make a complaint of a violation of their rights.

Another strike is the country where the immigrant came from. If he emigrated from a Western European country, he may be given a benefit of the doubt as the law officer would be trying to live up to the "civilized" standard he had been brainwashed to believe. Sometimes, the country of immigration could work against the European immigrant; if the officer is distraught or had a bad experience from that country on a previous vacation or encounter, for example.

But for a black immigrant who does not smile often to cover his hurts, his fate is really in the hand of God to get justice. The color of the law officer does not matter; the black immigrant gets shafted double. The white or Caucasian law officers may on rare occasions show some sensitivity. But the black law officers for reasons best known to them often show little or no sensitivity at all. But while they would not readily tell the black immigrant, the black law officers would make the situation of the black immigrant harder. This is also not unconnected with the false sense of superiority the black officers feel over their black brothers from across the seas. This may have been fueled by brainwashing too through images shown or discussed on television by half-baked "experts" on little known subjects or peoples.

They believe that people or immigrants from oppressed areas of the world should not complain when their rights are violated in the United States by law enforcement agents. It seems to be ingrained in many unscrupulous elements wearing the respectable badges of law enforcement that poor immigrants should not complain. The search for freedom, progress, and personal advancement are the reasons these immigrants came to the United States of America. No one would advocate that the black immigrants violate the law. What one is asking is that they (black immigrants) be accorded basic human respect under the law. But many immigrants have come to meet with very hostile hosts in segregated neighborhoods. Moreover, the facade of flashy smiles and high-pitched hello has really come home to roost with the black immigrants. It all means a definition of space and turf but certainly not to come any closer unless specifically stated. Just because a guy smiles and holds conversations with you as in other parts of the world and gives you a telephone number do not mean he wants to be your friend. It is often orchestrated, and the immigrants are better off alone than getting close to such homeboy or girl.

Many immigrants have fallen victim of their previous home country's ethics and cultures. When it comes to love affairs in the USA, the rules and definition of boundaries are unwritten, but nonetheless understood. Unfortunately for immigrants, the rules are the same here. Even when they are verbalized, they can be tricky. Feelings are not usually deeply felt here. They are orchestrated and acted as in the movies with no bearing on realities. Emotions are not to be felt too deeply, or the immigrant could leave himself or herself wide open and vulnerable. The areas of emotion have no color mark and no differentiation. The application is the same on all immigrants. It is actually never differently applied to born in the USA, but the natives are better equipped to deal with it since they have been exposed to such treatments since their adolescence. This latter piece had been kept hidden from the strangers to the USA and presented as a shocking behavior once exposed as in a drama acted upon. Some others born in the USA would even swear to the absence of such behavior from their own region of birth or upbringing, thereby shielding the country from facing up to the ills of the society. And God help the immigrant if he should voice a criticism of the people he was led to believe were wholesome by foreign editorial news broadcasts. He or she would be told to return to his native country if he or she doesn't like it here. This is easier said than done. The inability to take criticism kindly, however constructive, had been and continues to be the Achilles heel of decadence afflicting the ones born in the USA from their birth to adulthood. Hence, the children running away despite the opportunities. This phenomenon has no color boundaries.

Therefore, no matter the anecdotes ever concocted to deal with the decadence in America, none would find its mark in correcting this endemic anomaly. The psychologists, the majority of whom are nonparents themselves, have argued on speech making and conversations with children. This is all well and good, as good as it gets. But children are of different makeup. Hence, the upbringing must follow different patterns and nonconventional routes. Because the advice given in the past, and continues to be offered, has proven useless in fixing this decadence, this has enveloped the country and makes the future bleak at best for the children.

The effect of drug addiction continues to be felt and hidden as much as possible by the average Caucasian while the African Americans readily admits to the effect and its impact on the society. From the conservative South, Midwest, and Western states, the worst cover-up comes to light. They resorted to the Bible as the only way out while the preacher is already drug addicted and preaches behind a mask.

The reactions of the politicians on both sides of the aisle of U.S. politics are fun to watch. Each politician from each of the major political parties, continues to offer no solution while accusing the executive branch of the government of ineffective measures at fixing the drug problem of

America. The fact is the thin skins of Americans in accepting criticisms from their infancy generally, however constructive, is the culprit for the drug addiction epidemics, which they try to export overseas so that they (Americans) could point to "weaker beings" and accuse the same of bringing drug addiction to the USA as in the AIDS epidemic. After all, the Americans are "wholesome" without guile. All other people are the "violent" ones! Only Americans, and perhaps their British cousins, are the only "peace loving people on the face of the earth." Forget about slavery; forget about Hiroshima and Nagasaki. Forget about forceful invasion of other nations' territories under one pretense or another to "keep the world safe" for all. What garbage!

The fact is, the white Anglo-Saxon method of children's upbringing based on the Victorian-era philosophy of lying to oneself has been wrong headed as the method of shooting red men from the hip as depicted in those Wyatt Earp movies. The only teacher now is the tube. I mean the television. What needs to be done is to devise methods to teach the Americans from their infancy to adulthood on how to take constructive criticisms even from black or African immigrants even if they emigrated from impoverished nations. Now we have the computer and the Internet—God help us all!

The reconstruction of Americans must begin at once to include non-Caucasians and non- Jewish Americans or immigrants. No one has a monopoly on intelligence. Discouragement of racial discrimination, and discrimination based on countries of origin and emigration must not elude this great country, the opportunity to redeem herself in the eyes of the world. Those born in the USA have a lot to learn from the rest of the world and vice versa.

CHAPTER 8

American Fronts on Knowledge and Intelligence

The age of doctor-feel-good had been on for too long. From infancy, children have been made to feel good under any circumstances, and with any types of behavioral pattern. This has been an attempt not to damage the self-esteem of the child in accordance with early psychological findings. There was the Piaget theory of early child development, and there was Freud's phallic developmental stage theory which culminates in the Oedipus complex, setting the stage for intrafamily violence. These theories originated from the European intellectual vault. As if these are not enough, add Carl Jung, Kafka, and Friedrich Nietzsche with his already difficult situation of the overman psychology, and every Caucasian in America thinks he is God and incapable of being dead no matter the dangers he or she exposes himself or herself.

Thank goodness the racial policy, the subtle or overt discrimination against people of color, has continued to fuel the premise of superiority! Both the government and businesses continue to finance the premise that labor has to be on the backs of blacks or non-white immigrants. Problems, which would have been solved many years back, would be allowed to continue unsolved rather than involve the input of nonwhite or African immigrants. The color of the skin is very important to an ignorant population in determining the intelligence and content of character of an individual. So is ethnicity.

With this backdrop, everyone born in the USA feels he knows more than the nonwhite or African immigrant, especially with their distinct accents in spoken English. Even when they know nothing of the subject matter, they feel obliged to question the expertise of the qualified immigrant who is certified by the authorities in the United States and who perhaps had to prove their knowledge and mastery of their professions three times over the born in the USA who are in the same fields of knowledge. What's worse is when the African immigrant, expert of his or her profession, repulses this wanton and blatant disrespect, however diplomatically, he or she is labeled a hostile professional.

This uneven treatment stems from the racial discrimination and assessments of the U.S. policy which nitwits would latch strongly on to, to prove the essence of their own worth on the face of the earth.

Even with the learned professional Caucasians of the same expertise as this African or African American professional, and who actually know the superiority of the African professionals, they continue to live the lie unless faced with a helpless situation. Even with that, they adopt a pugilist stance and appear to have lost their sense of speech or awareness. Who cares as long as you have the unfair advantage over a defenseless fellow human being? But the law of Karma still operates. Boomerang is still in vogue! Therefore, let no one asks why me when he or she is fed with the food he or she prepared!

CHAPTER 9

Religious Persuasions in America

Even before I left the shore of Africa, I have known of American missionaries. These were Christians who had come to spread the "word of God" to a "backward African people." What an irony! The quest or the belief was purchased with money. First, they bring money to build educational institutions—schools, hospitals, and maternity centers. Then other conditions come in, such as the offer of employment in these institutions provided that the religious doctrine is accepted. In fact, acceptance of whichever sect of Christian faith was mandatory to be eligible and accepted in the leadership and administration of the various institutions for the African native of these lands. In the name of religion and Christianity, in particular, the Americans were able to recruit the natives faster than any other religion was ever able to do.

I suspect that the many denominations fashioned out here of the Christian faith was borne out of the desire to enrich the founders who are often able to take advantage of the nonprofit tax code for religious freedom. If you listen to these Christian preachers, you would think they were in with the Divine Father when the earth and all other humans were created. They each claim to be directly chosen and anointed after being saved from lives of transgression, crimes, and/or drug addiction. They regard anyone who would not bow to their brand of worship and belief as sinners who had not been saved and who had not known the proper path to the Almighty God to which each of them is privy exclusively. Funny, they speak of religious freedom, but they never respect or are willing to tolerate other religious persuasions.

This may have had a racial tint to it from the beginning of the founding of this nation. Witness the robbing and the seizure of lands belonging to the Indian natives of the land before the mass slaughtering of these people in the name of Christianity. It is interesting to hear of the stand of these same people for peaceful existence. What a crock!

I often wonder if Christianity would be chosen as their religion had the symbol not been depicted as a blue-eyed, straight-nosed, wavy-haired Caucasian nailed on the cross by the hated Jews. By hanging on to their religion, the Jews had drawn the wrath of the Christian Caucasians. Witness Hitler's pogrom in Germany. And when the Jews in America got together and through meticulous organization became a credible force to reckon with, the faith of the Caucasian became the Judeo-Christian faith, especially having had to deal with the fact that Jesus Christ was a Jew.

New territories must be conquered and new set of people of nonwhite races must be humiliated "in the name of Jesus Christ." First, the people must be small number and defenseless. Once that occurs, it would be a field day in the name of Christianity. Such defenseless people must be subjugated to the whims and caprices of these "Christian" people. The wrath of these "Christians" fell on the Palestinians who had refused to be annihilated but who nonetheless have been proving to the Caucasians of Western Europe and America that their religion is not monolithic. In fact, they have among them those who subscribe to Christianity with the same ferocity as the Caucasians' initial hate for the Jews. But because the Islamic religion, which the Caucasian Christians and their hirelings consider an affront to their religion, was first identified with the Palestinians, the reconciliation with the new facts of the Palestinian is slowly sinking in. But the southern USA Anglo-Saxon Christians who have not read the facts are still sticking to their old doctrine of hate and intolerance of other religious beliefs.

Many blacks or African Americans have suffered this fate. Their religions from Africa was beaten out of their brains––so also were their names––throwing a whole people into confusion after being stripped of their identities. To escape certain death, many slaves had accepted the

Caucasian owners' names and of course his religion which completed the total subjugation.

Today as it was in those days, any African American citizen with the features of the old line of slavery who attempts to choose another religion other than Christianity handed down to him or her is viewed as confrontational and refusing to accept the Caucasian leadership. Many times, the irony of the situation is that the other African Americans would view any brother or sister veering off the Christianity path with disdain. Sometimes not so much disdain than envy for that brother or sister daring to refuse to be a slave anymore in this modern time and leaving the others in perpetual enslavement to the master.

What has now been observed of the African Americans of Islamic religion persuasions is their apparent portrayal of themselves as the true believers and the chosen followers of the prophet Mohammad even more than the Arabs and the Persians who brought the religion to them. Some things never change in the psyche of those born in the USA of all creeds.

But what I suspect is that religious affiliation for those born in the USA had nothing to do with the belief in divine greatness or supreme being because what else would be greater than the flag of the American nation to which every American must pledge allegiance and defense? Religious affiliation in essence here has to do with the holier-than-thou attitude and independence of the founders and those who carry on after them in any industry called church ministry. When you are the reverend, you become the head of a group of people whom you could hold sway over. Sometimes the heavy handedness of some of the church leaders would lead to creation of more splinter Christian denomination churches. Sometimes the transgressions of the church leaders and ministers had led to disillusion and creation of the worship of the Satan which these worshippers see no difference from the deeds of the Christian churches and its members at large.

The worship of Satan or devil in the USA is the territory of the rebellious whites or Caucasians born in the USA. The religion gave them an excuse to commit heinous crimes. Many even spill over into the membership of Aryan clan or the Neo Nazi group. But it will not be true to say all Americans do not believe in the Supreme God Almighty. Who else had been the protector of defenseless African Americans and, by extension, the Africans for all these generations? It is only those, among these defenseless people, with a figment of imagination of greatness who had developed amnesia about how far they have come through their fathers and mothers and their grandparents.

When the white church leaders especially from the southern and western sections of America do speak against "Christian" persecution in third-world countries, they do so in self-serving terms. They often behave as if they are the pure and "saved" deliverers of the people only to bring them over here and subjugate them again. Or they follow the old ways of getting a foothold in the third-world countries in the name of religion and fomenting division of people along religious lines. Money had always been the ammunition or weapon of choice of the Christian religion. And the "free" gifts have fooled the people, making them lose more than they ever received economically and spiritually and psychically.

Unfortunately, the Caucasians pass the racist opinions and remarks to their children, creating an ignorant nation. Because of the frail egos of the already-brainwashed Caucasians, every failure in their respective lives is blamed on the black or impoverished people. And because of their vulnerability and inability to compete on a one-to-one, level fields, they (Caucasians) spend inordinate time in scheming and dividing the nonwhite people against each other. Since they possess the economic monopoly, the people who appear Caucasian or white reward the foolish or sometimes spineless or timid black people against the more expressive or assertive and otherwise intelligent ones in the community, in the schools, and at workplaces.

We may pretend and editorialize as much as possible, but the longer we continue to sweep this shortcoming under the rug, the quicker the calamity, *which will result from the suppressed anger and consume the entire people.* Even those who think they cannot be touched personally *would be touched* through their children's actions. These children may be destroyed both physically and spiritually and thereby ending the progeny which this nation and most other nations cherish.

Yes, America, despite its bravado, is still afraid to face the demon that lives in its soul, and that demon called racism will sooner or later eat its heart up. Yes, she inherited the hate from her cousins in Europe––Britain and Germany––but she has the unique leadership to annihilate the racist gene. The brainwashed "superiority" complex makes it difficult for the born-in-the-USA Caucasians to deal with non-European or Caucasian names. Exception to the rule is the Jewish or Hebrew names which they grudgingly pronounce well for fear of being labeled an anti-Semite. The fear of the anti- Semitism is a result of the Jewish economic power in the media and other areas, which they deeply resent privately. The recognition they (Caucasians) gave to the Jewish accomplishment is owed to the Jewish economic power in the media and commerce.

What is sometimes horrifying is that the Jewish community would sometimes join with the same people who despise them for being the people they are against a defenseless black population. And also some ignorant blacks join forces against the born-in-the-USA African American who decide to assume their ancestral African names or their religious names other than the Christian names or slave owners' names given forcibly to them and carried around their neck from generation to generation. Some retain the names as a testimony to the suffering of their parents in the hands of their owners or as a testimony to a claim of the land. Whichever way anyone looks at it, it never gave him or her (African American) a better shake over the Caucasian in spite of their superiority of argument. But when they fail to close ranks with their brothers and sisters from across the Atlantic Ocean with the thick African accent, the born-in-the-USA African loses all his or her grace and defenses.

CHAPTER 10

American Attractions to Peddled Products

You almost want to burst out laughing when you see the way people of America are taken to the cleaners by peddlers of various products. The laughter is not for a funny spectacle. The laughter is that of embarrassment for a people who always pride themselves on their intelligence and know-how. What I have never been able to figure out is how a people could allow himself or herself to be blinded by psychological racism translated into reality. Before long, it became part of the whole makeup of a population.

The aspect of racism was mainly the domain of the Caucasians. These people with very frail egos have to be psychologically whipped for self-esteem until it is translated into dangerous aggression and violence. You can make a lot of money if you're a Caucasian and a fast talker before they get wise to the acts. Often you get the full benefit of trust first before doubts follow. But for a nonwhite, the doubt and disbelief from the Caucasian or the brainwashed nonwhite follower is the first order. Even after it is proven that the nonwhite or African descendant peddler of product is true, the embrace of the product is slow, tepid, and suspicious. With this attitude, they'd rather get the destruction from the dangerous product peddled by their own kind, or so goes the saying.

Many Caucasians in the USA have been taken to the cleaners and their death by many Caucasian professionals in different fields of expertise––law, medicine, research sciences, and television show people.

This product peddling and dishonesty started from elementary school. The Caucasian teacher shows undue favoritism to some Caucasian kids with normal aptitude even if they are mediocre or average students at best. This kind of favoritism leads to the making of incompetent leaders of organizations, corporations, and government departments. The era of President Clinton seems to be changing attitudes howbeit with a lot of difficulties. For a change, the American Caucasian is coming to grips with reality that intelligence is not his domain alone. If anything, the Caucasian is no superman or Tarzan any more than any black man or African sitting on top of human intelligence or knowledge. What is offered here is the realization that whatever progress has been made is achieved by the collaboration of the people regardless of their racial backgrounds, claims of die-hard racists notwithstanding.

The sad situation is the joining of truly intelligent Caucasians with the die-hard racists in fostering the lie of racial superiority against their better judgment and knowledge of facts. But I do suspect that they do so because of their own personal frame of reference. Being Caucasians or whites, as they like to call themselves, they (the Caucasian intellectuals) could not bring themselves to swallow their pride and correct the anomalous assertions from Adolf Hitler down who have been made them to swallow their words time and time again.

The young ones of the Caucasian extraction must realize that their racist grandparents lied to them when they told them that they are superior to other races of people. They lied to them when they told them of their supremacy. No human of any race is supreme over the other. God Almighty, the creator of all living and nonliving beings, is the only supreme being over man. It was never revealed to anyone whether God is of any complexion known to man except in the image of the figment of individual's imagination.

The mentality of racial preference exhibited by Anglo-Saxons and other Caucasians spilled into the religious worship, enriching in no small measure the white preacher with majority following and of success in the South and western regional sectors of the USA where racial segregation is overtly pronounced or promoted, the discrimination law notwithstanding. No wonder then why the black churches are flourishing too. If this mentality begins from the least likely area, no wonder the endemicity of crime, hate, and drug addiction threatening to consume the entire nation.

The Republican Party politicians love to claim to be the vanguard for the American Christian way. Now we know which way they believe in and what they all stand for. Instead of leading the people down the path of enlightenment, they speak with forked tongues and retain the people in ignorance. The Southern Democrats have not fared much better than their colleagues. They have allowed themselves to be blackmailed as black or poor people lovers, gay lovers, and liberals as if there's something decadent in caring for the less privileged, which is, along with promoting equity for the privileged overall, what the politicians are sent to the U.S. Congress and State Houses to do in the first place.

In the end, for genuine products developed by nonwhite or African Americans to be widely acceptable, the front spokesperson might as well be a Caucasian. Such is the world we live in now but it's changing, but the turning may seem slow. The brainwashing seems to have been complete, and every effort to reinforce the phenomenon is pursued relentlessly. Many leaders of African nations are muzzled with corruption to the detriment of their countries' prestige in the world. Worse still, the commodities used for the sustenance of those poor countries can be further undervalued or devalued, forcing these countries into bankruptcy should the leaders of the third world or nonwhite nations refuse to be corrupted.

Wherever there's poverty, the people lose their orientation to focus on scientific or economic progress in favor of the immediate need for food. We have witnessed in the third world how the agricultural products of some of these nations were chemically destroyed through deceitful claim of chemical insecticide products developed and financed by Western government led by the USA. Cocoa is one example of such product from African countries that is losing favor against the cocoa plantations owned by the Caucasians in Brazil and other tropical countries in South America.

CHAPTER 11

On the Problem of Stable Family

The inability to have stable families in the USA has nothing to do with the individuals who suddenly find that they cannot live together but more to do with the speed by which they've decided to stay together in the first place. If there's anything the people of the USA are deprived of the most, it is their freedom. Freedom of association, enshrined in the U.S. Constitution, is most flagrantly denied to individual citizens by the same group of citizens who would shout the loudest about freedom. Many a young Caucasian American boy or girl has been prevented from exercising that right of freedom to associate with whoever they feel like associating with by peer pressure, groups willing to keep people separate and estranged from each other by artificial barrier of skin complexion.

Only where some Caucasian children broke free from that chain do they discover liberty, to the chagrin of the rest of their ignorant folks. In fact, the Caucasian consider it a betrayal if any other racial members find love and companionship in any other race or ethnic group not resembling Caucasians. They don't get angry. In fact, they approve howbeit silently if a Caucasian bonds with primates and dogs rather than human of another racial group. But there's nothing absurd in this reaction. It is the makeup of the Caucasian. The character is entrenched in the need to control and shore up a frail ego.

There is even more competing egos when the Caucasians are married couples. More often, they cannot allow equality in their relationship.

Hence the need to visit the marriage counselors more often than they would enjoy each other's company.

The sense of romantic interplay conveyed to the born-in-the-USA Caucasian male is only through the media. Before the age of television and movies, it was through the imagination of the solitary fiction novelists. I have observed that the whole expression of love of those born in the USA borders on display of their insecurity necessary for mutual reinforcement and assurance. Any break in the reciprocity for air by any of the participants in this display is construed as loss of confidence and a break of the confidence fictitiously constructed. Once they declare to love and cherish each other, the trigger of distrust goes into effect. From then on, wherever the male goes, it must be accounted for. He must continue to affirm his love to his woman verbally even if he doesn't mean it. And he must make love on demand, and if he cannot perform this rite, there will be an alarm of probable infidelity or loss of interest in the mate or, worse still, a suspicion of homosexuality or impotence, which is at the end of the list.

The latter suspicion may lead to rejection of advances when the male does come around to his female counterpart. The rejection often leads to in-house fighting and flow of bad bloods, cumulating in divorce, separation, and court-ordered restrictions. Since many in this great land have never been taught to accept personal responsibility except in a show of chivalry, their frustration in love affairs often finds expression in various aggressive modes. This can come in forms of children being held hostage or one of the frustrated parties stalking the other or, worse still, finding comfort in strengthening of racist and radical group memberships.

The latter crime phenomenon could be deciphered from the atrocities committed against foreign nationals in foreign wars. The former crimes have led to senseless killings and serial killing scenario of innocent people. Usually, in the racial hate expression, these blame the other races for their problem. In the most unjustified situation, you find the frustrated Caucasian blaming his hard luck on the black immigrant or African American "success." Envy and anger at the apparent ability of the black man's ability to convert deprivation to "acceptable" norm, rationalized and managed. Still, this is not enough; the Caucasian wishes the black man would just disappear, which never solves his problems. Unfortunately, the fixation of the Caucasian on the enormous residence of the black man has been noted and recorded all over Western Europe where such racial presence had been recorded.

Reaction to foreign news often finds its mark in the frustrated Caucasian egos. Male or female (the female often echoing the male frustration in attempts to show loyalty or solidarity rather than rely on their own better judgments would instinctively get vituperative against the foreign enemy even if they do not understand the issues at stake. Many of the policymakers and intelligence operatives for the government may be suffering from this ego bruising and frustration in the love department.

Unfortunately, the absence of money or source of it in all families contribute immensely to the destabilization of the family institution. For the Caucasian born in the USA, this situation is unacceptable. Coupled with other afflictions in this ethnic racial group, absence of money or source of it usually aggravate the unstable relationships. The need to be a "Jones" continues to aggravate the precarious stability of marriage relationship. The relationship with the absence of money and source more often than not aggravates beyond imagination where children are added to the scenario. As already expressed, exception is never the rule. The Caucasians have a very low threshold for tolerance, which they preach on other racial ethnic groups of the world. They often preach docility and peace to other racial or ethnic groups of the world, which they could never accept or abide by.

Most other ethnic groups, especially immigrants, could manage in America with the barest minimum of resources and maintain healthy relationships. Their strength is found in the hope of their future mostly through their children's eventual success and survival. On the other hand, the afflictions visited on the African Americans, coupled with the conflicting stick-and-carrots phenomena, have confused the population to the extent that even with the African resilience reservoir, the maintenance of relationship becomes daunting. This often presents buoyancy for the egos of the born-in-the-USA Caucasian and often cited to justify their continuous campaign of calumny and indignation against an innocent population.

Often, because of the ultimate referral of cases of indiscrimination and deprivation to the Almighty God's justice, a powerless immigrant African picks up pieces of life left to him and moves on. The apparent happiness found in hope for the future is cited for the justification of the treatment handed down to the nonwhite immigrant, ingratiating themselves on the "correctness" of their action.

Who would know better about injustice than the immigrant who had emigrated from a difficult homeland? But what irks him is that he was totally caught off guard by the life he came to face in the USA. This was not what was told to him. He was expecting utopia. But he soon learned and his adaptation to the environment has been phenomenal if only limited in wherever he could go and what benefit he could attain. He has to fight both the *Caucasian overlords* and the *crablike underlings* of the those *born in* the USA, the ones below the ladder in the hierarchy of skin color gradient. *Unfortunately,* some *children* of the oppressed people of *color,* mostly the females, choose a path of skin bleaching, hoping to erase the only pigment of pride and protection of their race from nature—the melanin pigment—in order to fit into the model which the Caucasian created as "fair" complexion.

It will be difficult to understand what is expected of a population of people whose male members are plotted against from the time they are born until their adulthood and consequent death. These male compatriots are denied jobs in the majority having been plotted against, e.g., dishonorable discharge from the armed forces no matter how heroic their services, with PTSD, drug addiction et al., and trumped-up charges of crime resulting in prison terms. Only a handful had gotten a reprieve through some pro bono Caucasian attorneys. This is just a handful of cases. Think of what had happened to the thousands with the pugilist Caucasian prosecutors and "law" enforcement agents looking at one straight in the eye and lying like hell. They (the born-in-the-USA Caucasians) maintain their stories of "correctness" because the laws would support their deliberate lies for the distortion that had been brought to the lives of these repressed population.

With the males of the African American population stripped of every natural human dignity and largely incarcerated by trumped up charges, there is no wonder then that the upbringing of the children of that population would be impaired. I am not excusing any misfit behavior here, but I am calling the born-in-the-USA Caucasian and his cousins from across the Atlantic to own up to the modern-day crime against all the nonwhite or non-Caucasian populations. The calculated precision of the crime is so rampant that its endemicity is generic. The inculcation of the character in the genome of the Caucasian youth seems to have an on switch, at a point in time, of their growing young years and remains turned on for life, only shelved through internal moral struggle. Those Caucasians who managed to shelve or extinguish or turn off the racist switch remain targets of their fellow Caucasians for ridicule and trumped-up charges sometimes worse than the nonwhite "enemies" to be taught a lesson.

With the aforementioned premises, how can a male African American take himself or be taken seriously in relationships? With no premise of respectability surrounding his persona, from his young life, there is no wonder then that his dignity is constantly questioned both by himself and a dispassionate observer. Never mind the professional status of the individual black man and how much money he has made as a result of such attainment. The truth is the aura of dignity has been stripped off his persona as he was growing, and despite his attainment professionally, he continues to be made to feel powerless and hopeless to influence any trend except to follow it the way it was scripted by some Caucasian designer however wrongheaded such designs may be.

It would have been logical for the African-Americans to join forces with their kinsmen from Africa to fight the stripping of their personal dignity but these Born in The USA African Americans with Anglo-Saxon names regard such suggestions coming from their Cousins across the Atlantic ocean as big insults possibly coming from age-long brain washing. Besides, the Caucasian has told him that he was lucky to be born in the USA. Scores of television footage have been brought home to support the "lucky" assertions. The born-in-the-USA African Americans have for years been wrongly informed of their "leadership" over the rest of the nonwhite and African populations only to be rated lower by the designers of the brainwash, thereby precipitating confusion and confrontation with the natural allies in the common fight against oppression and discrimination. Ideas from their brothers from Africa, however correct and logical, are given lukewarm reaction. So also are ideas brought by brothers from the Caribbean or West Indies who may have confused them (African Americans born in the USA) at first because of the common Caucasian names shared. But as soon as identified as not from the fold of those born in the USA, the thought of learning from their own brothers and sisters and not from the less-knowledgeable Caucasians seem to rob them (those born in the USA) of a nonexistent self-pride.

CHAPTER 12

Recognizing the Difference of the Genders

I have written earlier on how women have been coerced into supporting every bias and fear ever concocted by men of every race, creed, and ethnic group. The women do so out of loyalty to their men or out of fear of reprisal from the dominant male psyche or out of peer pressure of other women who already succumbed to the ideas of their men. The truth is that most women are generally very thoughtful and revisit their positions about a lot of things no matter their attachment to these positions. They can be made to follow a new good line of reasoning and logic unlike most men who have deep feelings of self–righteousness. You will agree with me when you still see a lot of women packed in a church or synagogue where the priest has been convicted of some impropriety every Sabbath. You will be surprised when women, having convicted a suspect, continues to be plagued by doubts of the judgment rendered as part of a jury in a court of law.

Racism or segregation was never part of a woman's makeup somatically and psychically whatever fear or idea of fear that has had been put there by men. Therefore, until the women truly liberate themselves from mental slavery, they will never be free. A woman looks forward to marrying a stronger man for protection and to do the hard chores around the home. Or they do so for financial security for the type of lifestyles built in their heads. Yes, women would rather choose to live with any man their gut feelings want them to live with. But with the control being exercised over the Caucasian and Caucasian-wannabe women, their bondage mentally and physically and psychologically is now complete. Never mind what they verbalize. These women are not free. They invariably are jealous of the ones brave enough to step out and marry outside their races (which still needs further analysis).

Today, marriage outside the Caucasian race for the born-in-the-USA women of Caucasian descent means getting the man she can control or feel superior to while getting the gentle largess and considerate devotion in abundance. Sometimes, her built-in lack of trust of one another transmits to the men of other races or cultures. This in many ways, because of the obvious insecurity and inferiority complex toward other women of non-Caucasian race, often lead to the breakdown of the otherwise perfect union. The coldness at home and constant interrogation and desire to cut the non-Caucasian man from his friends and relatives would finally drive the wedge through the union. Moreover, the non-Caucasian or foreign male must either have accomplished his professional career before meeting the born-in-the-USA Caucasian woman, or else put such ambition at bay or it may be another reason for friction.

This, by the way, is not racial. Women just want to have their cake and eat it at the same time. Most African American women who grew up in the USA would do the same things as their born-in-the-USA Caucasian compatriots. The only difference is that against a black or African immigrant, they would over play their hands until they get a rude shock of resistance. Because African American women have always been placed in advantageous positions over their men by the U.S. system of government, they often feel that they had to ride their men overtly. Eventually, they evoke uncontrollable anger from the African American male whose ego had been and still is bruised by the unjust system.

The relationship of the Caucasian male with the African American woman is peculiar. In fact, more of master-servant or more of the master's condescending treatment of his subject is the accurate description. It has never been of equal partnership. But despite the immense intelligence a woman possesses, she loses all when she allows her selfish interest to interfere with her reasoning. Many born-in-the-USA women of all races who had children with recent immigrant men have had the children taken away to foreign land, never to be seen again, and when those children do return at adolescence or as adults, there's no telling of their confusion and bitterness against their parents and, consequently, the world. Whenever the foreign fathers are made to leave their children to the care of the mothers, the society is made to bear the brunt of their anger of miseducation. The born-in-the-USA women––quick to utter the phrase of "who needs you?"––nevertheless become dependent on the state, which is very impersonal to say the least. Usually, only luck would see the children through if they never become the statistics of failure.

The only difficulty I have with the born-in-the-USA women is their attempt to try to export their failed methods of raising children to other countries, particularly Latin America and Africa. In these foreign lands, the only problem they seem to have and which seems intractable is poverty. Once these countries of the third world have sensible and selfless leaders, their problems would be solved. Many an African American woman born in the USA has been miseducated and misdirected by the system. Many of these women of African descent have been brainwashed to always only look up to and only respect the Caucasian handouts. Many have copied the lifestyles of the Caucasian women to their own peril. Many have tried to bleach their skins or tone it to be acceptable to Caucasians or Caucasian lover homeboys. Either way, both victims suffer from identity crisis.

Now that the Cherokee Indians have been passed aside and despised, no one of the possible descendants would own up to the heritage except where advantageous to themselves and for spite. But the most striking thing about the born-in-the-USA women is their similarity with all other women of the world. They are so diverse and brilliant and caring and motherly despite the tough exterior they project. The tough exterior pose has been thrown on them by the pressure of life in this land of plenty. It is ironic that their femininity is being stripped off them by the same confused bisexual Caucasian men of power in the USA.

It is very important for the born-in-the-USA women to understand the hypocritical solidarity of the born-in-the-USA Caucasian male, especially when the women are in conflict with their foreign non-English-speaking black men or other men of color. They must reclaim their essence and femininity and charm. Reality has brought it home to them that their children need their fathers for personal stability and growth psychically and psychologically, regardless of the financial endowment surrounding them. They need the fathers for their stability and completeness. We have seen the evidence that the absence of that part of nurturing affect both the male and female children up to their adult life span.

Women have always been curious naturally. They are more sociable naturally than men who on the other hand are more lonesome and require a social contract in order to be sociable. This is because men, for some unknown reasons, feel that they need overt competition in all things however trivial. Many men of all races do not know, for some reasons, their limitations of mastery of some tasks. Their (male) ambitions run wild even when they know little of the ambitious they're pursuing. The motivation seems to be amassing of wealth and exercising of control over other men even when they do not know how. Many times, this last item has led to revolt and rejection of authority where such men have reigned. But for democracy, the world would be full of despotic dictators.

Occasionally, women who want to mold themselves in men's role may assume this unfortunate trait, but invariably, we see through them as they are—usually harder on other women and neglect their concerns. But chauvinism has had chilling effect on male ego development. History of events all over the world has shown that it is more in Caucasians who run around the world looking for conquests.

Finally, the perceptive instincts of women and their superior ability in some instances to see the machination of the opposition against Bill Clinton convince them that despite the crime, the punishments would have been far in excess as to deprive the nation of his services. Whenever the women dance to the tune of the hypocritical conservative males, they lose big time, either because of lack of self-conviction or education and identity. The feelings of black men and women against new immigrants are understandable. They have endured hundreds of years of suffering, and still counting. Seeing new immigrants coming in to reap what they perceive as their hard-worn gain, however modest, most African Americans sometimes vent their frustrations against the wrong or innocent people.

What is unknown to the African American, born in the USA, is that most immigrants from the developing nations have borne the brunt of the suffering, which translates into the comfort of the Americans. The immigrants from those third-world nations have been paid less than lowest wages paid to the lowest or minimum pay in the USA. Their lifestyles invariably, except in a few cases, mirror the lives of the downtrodden Americans. God knows what web the CIA and other agencies of the USA weave to keep the people of the third world in perpetual poverty.

CHAPTER 13

On the Population Makeup of the USA

There are fewer topics that occupy the minds of the Caucasians in the USA more than the population distribution. Caucasians have always known of the strength in numbers. After all, their slip of their hold on power in the so-called third-world nations, which they colonized, has been because of the overwhelming population increase of natives in these countries. Witness South Africa, Zimbabwe, Angola, Mozambique, and Namibia where they maintained a presence for more than three to four hundred years only to lose power in the twentieth century to African owners of the land. But the Caucasian invaders of America are determined to prevent this situation from happening on their stranglehold on power. After all, the founding fathers of the USA tried and succeeded to some extent to annihilate the Indians they met here. Unlike the Indians, the Africans waited and studied these invaders and after initial resistance settled to master his ways and beat him at his games without surrendering his own cultures, which won the land back for him.

This brings us to the point of Caucasian clamor for population. There is no other topic in the modern times that evolves so much emotion than this topic. And there's none that brings forth much controversy and confusion even from those who believe in it. The topic stands in the way of life of the Caucasian and his genetic makeup no matter whether he believes in the principle or not. On the one hand is his freedom to do as he or she pleases from his or her time of birth and the responsibility being "imposed" on that freedom. On another point, is his or her desire to control his or her destiny and recognizing the character makeup to limit or restrict the need to increase the population at his or her own choosing. Coupled with this is the lifestyle he or she is being forced to adopt in order to be in the mainstream. Many born-in-the-USA Caucasians are gays or gays in the closet with less intense desire to raise children. Worse are the bisexual life styles, which tends to murk the distinctions. Like Huntington's disease, this phenomenon of homosexuality has been passed on different populations, which share genetic traits with Caucasians. This trait is only found in other parts of the world where there had been contact and shared parenthood with a Caucasian. I challenge anyone who could find the opposite to this assertion.

Back again to the subject of population, the frets and pants of the Caucasian have reached a feverish pitch. To be supplanted by a non-Caucasian population is a certain "death sentence." For them to live on the equal plane with others is anathema. A Caucasian, especially Anglo-Saxon Caucasian, thinks it is right for him to dominate other humans. He points to modern technology as his legacy, forgetting to state how he stole the ideas and how many nonwhite humans make the ideas a reality. I fail to understand how leadership or domination could be conferred to anyone simply by being a clever rogue and at the same time claiming a moral high ground. The reality of low birth rate among the Caucasians and the attending infertility of the female of this ethnic human have led to the wanton harassment of most female Anglo-Saxon Caucasian seeking abortion or intentions to terminate an unwanted pregnancy. The religious right wing Republican Party members are making abortion a litmus test for political office holding in the USA. The Democratic Party members who are from the so-called conservative South (a synonym with *prejudice* and is a racially biased region) are caught in the web. They recognize the reality of life and the sociological and psychological makeup of the American Caucasian, but because they are also Anglo-Saxons, they render themselves impotent by declining to mount challenges to the Republican right wing drive. There is no doubt that these latest frets stand to divide the Anglo- Saxon population as they fly in the face of the lifestyles of the population.

Other ways to reduce the population of the nonwhite must be devised! Projections of lower population of the American Caucasian citizens in key industrial states are out. By year 2025, more present minorities would share policy-making decisions on key issues of the nation.

One of those ways is the number of hysterectomy, or removal of uterus, procedures performed on the women of color across the United States of America. This procedure is not only carried out by Caucasian physicians but also by the wannabe non-Caucasian physicians. The wannabes' overriding reason is financial. They believe that the nonwhite women could mount little or no challenge to their practice, let alone successful challenge. Another method is the apparent reluctance to allocate anymore immigration quotas to the nonwhite world into this nation of immigrants, coupled with glutting the third-world nations with population explosion by tying any economic aid to these countries to abolition of abortion procedure for whatever reason. The adoption of investment in the future of the offsprings is late in embrace, but for a different reason.

With the harsh realities of life in the USA, the immigrant has developed sharper instincts and suspicion on everything from the use of the credit cards to the swallow of new medical pills. There will always be a few who would later learn the bitter lessons of their folly. Also, helping to increase the population of the immigrant nonwhite is the inability to afford the medical expenses available to Caucasians. Many have turned to the homeopathic medicine known to them in their home countries from where they immigrated to the USA. Their general state of good health, despite the denials of access, has often surprised mainstream medical establishments. But occasionally, they (non-Caucasian immigrants) fall victim when surgical procedures necessitate some remedies in their health. These unfortunate periods often result in the hysterectomies of their (nonwhite immigrants) young women who may be experiencing what medical people call metromenorrhagia. This condition is treatable in the hands of careful Geneticists. But because of prejudice and careless acts of butchery that leads to profuse bleeding are performed on these groups of valuable and hardworking citizens in the USA, the bleeding often leads to total abdominal hysterectomies.

The accents and some English-speaking imperfections and different non-English last names often give them away.

On paper, the policy of the U.S. government is evenhanded in intention. It is the executioners who bring their personal baggage of bias into the performance of their duties. Many other times, the need of the Caucasian to disturb the tranquility of the non-English speaking immigrants becomes paramount, often accusing them of child abuse in cases of normal disciplinary measures being taken by the immigrants on their children. These measures have served the people so well and have raised admirable model citizens. The model citizen's scenario often shatters the myth of the Caucasian uprightness. Even that model, however laudable, must not come from the non- Caucasian population. The Mongolian or Asian population could not be used as a model for upbringing implicitly. Since the phenomenon of domination was introduced, it is either one fault or the other found with vocal non-Anglo-Saxons. That is the unfortunate downside of life but given more intensity and credo by the imperialist Caucasian of Anglo-Saxon extraction. For centuries, the phenomenon had infected otherwise peaceful or primitive societies. Most other non- white societies have been allowed to progress at their own (Caucasian's) expense because of their obsession with black man's suppression and control. Most other non-white societies have thrived in order sociological ways than the Anglo Saxon ones. It is my honest belief that the world domination would stop when no nation would be able to overpower another. The world would come to its senses for mutual or world survival. Somehow this villainous instinct has become both generic and genetic in its transmission.

Population control must be continued. And a woman's right to bear or not to bear children must be respected. I think it is barbaric for anybody, let alone a group of Caucasian men who cannot have children, have never been fathers, could never be fathers, and could never have the tolerance and patience to raise children on their own dictate, to women because of their secret whims of increasing the Anglo-Saxon population at all costs. The women must bear children regardless, whether the pregnancy is of rape, of no love desire, or resulting in genetically impaired children. A pregnancy resulting from love and desire, no matter what, would still be loved by the carrier. This is the extent these racist individuals who are at the lowest sociological order of the human race, the real cavemen who have not been converted to modern living, would go. Forget the fact that they have money or have built some businesses. A single look at their pathetic personal lives would convince all doubters.

The pattern and policy at the business and edifice any of these racist conservatives owned or headed usually reflect the wrongheaded, deep-seated biases pent up over the years. And more often than not, such policies end up destroying the edifices however well started and no matter the height of "prestige" attained over the years. This is the classic case of the adage of cutting one's nose to spite one's face. After all, it is well known, and it has been accepted that the only thing that matters most to the Anglo-Saxon is the acquisition of wealth and money.

Christianity has been a useful weapon to foster this end in no measurable way. Many Anglo- Saxons lacking philosophy has been successful in personal family life by pursuing purely the Protestant work ethics. But they have squandered away whatever gains they made by pursuing a racist narrowly translated King James version of the Christian Bible.

In the end, the fear of being submerged by other people of non-Anglo-Saxon descent has often afflicted the Anglo-Saxon caveman from the beginning of time. This fear has consumed him; it has driven him to the point of preemptive aggression against otherwise peaceful population of other societies. The same fear has resulted in restlessness, which is carried in the genetic makeup. This has given rise to various neoplastic anomalies often observed in greater proportion among the people sharing their lineage and genetic makeup.

The introduction of Viagra, an anti-impotence drug, blew the lid wide open on the obsession and the thought process of the Anglo-Saxon and the Caucasian and wannabe ethnic groups. We now know, if not before, that love according to the human interpretation and more from the Caucasian standpoint means sexual intercourse performance and more of it from the standpoint of the women in this part on the world, and nothing else. This as it stands now validates Sigmund Freud's theory of Oedipus complex operating largely among the Caucasian population he studied and researched about. On the contrary, developmental stage in all human population does not go beyond the early developmental stage in the African population except for a spotty selection of African American families already drawn into the troubled Caucasian lifestyles.

The African success story of elimination of Oedipus complex effect may have to do with the open sophistication of discussion of problems brought *about by unaltered socialization among* the *people.*

CHAPTER 14

The Choice of Leadership in America

Democracy, the ingenious method of choosing a leader ever devised by man, led to the development and caring of societies, which have adopted it. Sometimes dictatorships have achieved the same. But democracy triumphed because the excesses of dictatorships could be kept in check, having been constrained within the constitution of the nations which adopted and practiced it. The United States of America in its rebellion against the British throne has perfected the democratic institution. But like all things, it has been abused occasionally and usually through the whims of the narrow-minded autocratic moneyman of racist intent. The rule of the majority, which has been used so successfully to legitimize most actions however bizarre, is now being feared to affect equality among people no matter their origin of descent.

After the initial success of democracy and the drawing of that magnificent document called the Constitution, racism reared its ugly head in the United States, leading to the denials of rights to people of color or non-Anglo-Saxon descent. After all, this country is supposed to be the "land of the "free" and the home of the brave." Freedom have never known any coloration. Neither does bravery nor courage.

These qualities are inalienable makeup of individuals regardless of which family or which country or nationality they originated from. Witness the achievements of many immigrants from diversified origins in spite of the obstacles encountered in the United States. But not all have been success stories. Many have paid with their dear lives for daring to dream and aspire to greatness because of the color of their skins. Many for the same reasons have been and are still incapacitated, for the atrocities have a way of incorporating itself in the genome and regenerating as if the same conditions of deprivation still exist. This is the psychological fallout of atrocities inflicted. It is this same psychology which directs the anger of the sufferers against the non-sufferers of the mentality of deprivation and fear of the Anglo-Saxons within the African American community and the African immigrants where the residuals seem to exist but nonetheless receding once dialogue is established.

If not managed, has anyone ever wondered how and why the leadership of the United States in its over two hundred years of independence despite its open-door policy proclamation have remained exclusively in the hands of the white Anglo-Saxon Protestants in large measures? It has never been by accident and it's no accident that the names of the United States presidents show its genealogy. The population must be made to reflect this philosophy either through rapid immigration from the other sisterly Anglo-Saxon nations or some measures of deprivation against an existing non-Anglo-Saxon population from participating in the franchise of choosing the leadership. The genetic frail egos are wanton indeed!

Other people of non-Anglo-Saxon outlook could be incorporated into the union to carry out the sinister acts against the nonwhite population by assimilation only to be cut to size lest their ambitions should be escalating beyond its proportional usage. The elaborate methods of choice of leadership usually bring into the open the ambitions of all people of such courage. It affords the orchestrators and manipulators of the process the opportunity to view firsthand who they are dealing with. It also affords the people the opportunity to view firsthand who they are dealing with. It also affords the people the opportunity to appraise the racist instincts in most of the Anglo-Saxon candidates who would come into the open competition for the leadership.

This is the ingenuity of the United States process. It is this elaborate system of perpetuation of the Anglo-Saxon's rule which makes the system second to none in the racial supremacy practice. Other European nations have developed foolproof systems, but theirs, while not in danger because of their "closed-door policies," do not have the elaborate contusions embedded within the U.S. process. Now, we know the system is not as open as proclaimed. The creation and maintenance of various intelligence agencies, viz., the CIA, Army Intelligence, OSS, FBI (a few of are clandestine) should have been the tipster of the secrecy enveloping the workings of the system. V. I. Lenin first mentioned the fifty families of the *Mayflower* Anglo-Saxon pilgrims who make sure the presidency of the USA reflects the descendancy of the early immigrant pilgrims. One thought it was just a communist hogwash. The family committee has since been increased to sixty to reflect the times.

The behaviors of several African governments never gave the immigrants a mouth to talk in the USA. While the pool of these immigrants show tremendous number of resourceful citizens capable of helping to move the inner cities of America forward as their new adopted home, their intelligence and contributions were never sought or outrightly or benignly ignored. Most born-in- the-USA African Americans would naturally feel that this is their turf, and hence an inner feeling of erosion and usurping of their rights should an African immigrant come to officiate over them. But they soon settle down to reason once the capability of the African immigrant has been proven. This constant ill-conceived idea of turfs has robbed the poor people of the leap forward for decades of determined leadership of the African immigrants. Since when has the accident of birth been the predetermination of the height an individual may attain? Yes, in the ignorant Old World of Europe and the caste system of India and Asian peninsula. But no more, I like to believe, in the present atmosphere of open intelligence. But what is disconcerting is the importance some racist conservatives attached to this accident of birth from all works. But to label rejectionists of these wrong assertions of the African descent as racists is to confuse the argument. It is an attempt to throw the unwary and uninformed into some unprepared identification. The rearing of the ugly heads of white supremacist groups in various areas of American states are results of fears that the population of the Caucasians would be submerged. But this is the United States with the safeguard system in place incapable of being shaken or disturbed by anyone no matter who is elected.

The fact of the matter is the greasing of the egos of the brainwashed born-in-the-USA Caucasians accustomed to giving orders and world of privilege and accomplishment with minimal capability. Encouragement and incentives abound to make a success of a Caucasian and a *Mayflower* descendant at that once he shows a willingness to continue to want the privilege thrown at him. Irrespective of the stumbles, he is given chances one after another. The same chances are never opened or given to nonwhite or African American fellow citizens. These so-called inferior citizens are expected to outperform the best Caucasian to earn the minimum grade for passing the task. Those who could not outperform the model Caucasian among the non-Caucasian immigrants are the ones who fall through the cracks of the system. The facts are now bearing the marks. The test of individual mettle, if really pursued, would make the leadership quota fall elsewhere from where it is now.

Just like the peddled commodities or products, so also must nonwhite talents be packaged and represented to the people of the United States by a Caucasian face to get acceptance by the Caucasian majority and sadly by some brainwashed nonwhites and blacks. But it would take some time for real progress on these fronts to be made by the nonwhite immigrants to recognize this aspect of deficient thinking process.

First, a lot of people would have to overcome the burden of day-to-day survival brought on them while pursuing meaningful and resourceful living. The playing field is not leveled. Never mind what Clarence Thomas and someone named Connerly said. Because they are married to Caucasian women, they become apologists for racial inequality. Deep down, these dark men wish they were white, and this questioning of their loyalty could stop. Just as some white or Caucasian men have turned their women with better intelligence to racial or white supremacists, so have some dark-skinned born-in-the-USA African male turned some African American women into self-doubting beings, devoid of pride in their race and self-worth of their existence.

By some irony of analogy, some black men born in the USA always claim that because they have their ancestors in slavery, they have come of age to remove such shackles from around their necks and their brains.

This has always been the reason they put forward to oppose anything that has to do with the advancement of their people from which they have previously benefited. What a confused set of people! The playing field is not yet leveled.

Needless it is to let them know that they have now in this modern time embraced the principle of slavery and, yes, mental slavery. They must think what their masters want them to think and say what must please their masters, or else they fall out of favor to be condemned. They have reentered the age of mental slavery in their attempt to be free from the same. The struggle for emancipation of the people is far from over. True independence has not yet been won. Racial defamation and discountenance continue to be the order of the day. These Uncle Toms continue to be the butts of jokes of both their white masters and the ridicule of their African American brothers and sisters. I hope to God that the financially successful never fall or be ruined by the same system that made them rich! How would they survive that turn of fate?

CHAPTER 15

Bring Them Down!

Many people never saw the connections. Some never read the designs. And many more succumbed to the barrage of repetitive rationale given for the fall from apparent grace of the very few prominent financially successful African Americans and other nonwhites born in the USA. Some of them may have survived the onslaught because they have the nonthreatening personality so necessarily needed for the Caucasian ego. Some unrepentant blacks may be despised because of their demand of respect until they are financially ruined by the unseen unity of purpose that saw to their demise.

Most born-in-the-USA nonwhite or African Americans would want to be known as American citizens period. This speaks volume of the class the African-Americans are held or viewed by the controlling class. The fact that the right to vote was never extended to these Americans until 1965, and even then it has to be recertified by an act of congress every two years would prove that the African-Americans have not been accepted as full and equal American citizens. This is despite their contributions to the development of the country. What is being advocated for the African-Americans is to own up to their glaring genetic heritage if nothing else. If there is anything more insulting to a people who had sacrificed everything including their heritage, I would like to know. With the other measures meted out to the black people born in the USA, the feeling of alienation cannot help being felt. Anyone who would blame the sensitivity of the people should try to wear their shoes for a change and feel the pain for size.

Yet the African resilience, which is the heritage of the African Americans, have helped them to weather this racial quagmire and prevent their total annihilation and destruction. This survivability has been a torn in the flesh of the Caucasian perpetrators of these evil designs. Because of the attention drawn to the confusion beleaguering the black community brought about by a combination of joblessness and drug addiction initiated sometimes during the enlistment in the armed forces and consequent dishonorable discharge to prevent them from holding responsible position in the civilian service thereafter, many a young African American not of proper understanding of these turmoil blame their own people who are the victims for their affliction. They, therefore, wish to absolve their oppressors of any crime perpetrated against their people. They embrace or refuse to react to evil appellation ascribed to the Caucasian who was born in the USA and the European American wannabe.

These innocent, ignorant, or opportunist African Americans are quickly embraced by the Caucasians who are always looking for ways by which to escape the guilt of their actions or deeds against their defenseless compatriots. They catapult the "ignorant" African Americans to the pinnacle of their professions. Their intelligences are selectively acknowledged to the detriment of others who truly deserve recognition in their various fields of endeavors.

None of the neophytes could do anything wrong as long as they continue to absolve the Caucasian who was born in the USA and their European counterparts of wrongdoing to their African American heritage and their African American development. But when moments of reflections come as it must on these cooperative, "conservative" African Americans, and they, having achieved certain degrees of financial or economic success, try to come back to the fold they long abandoned, they pay a very heavy price of ignominy.

Because of their longtime individual desire to please the powers that be to them, they burned their bridges behind them. And having been tolerated by the Caucasian as the tokens that must be endured to break the ranks and resolve of the common front being presented by the

African descendants, these few have managed to isolate themselves from their own natural constituents. They, therefore, without realizing it or having realized it too late have set themselves up for destruction one way or another. They are plucked out like feathers from the wing of a bird with no supporting cast and rendered useless unless they abandon that reflection and assertion of self, which momentarily overcame them. They must continue to live that existence of denial and enjoy the spoils therefrom. After all, this is what they always wanted, to be rich and live and have lives of no reflection or seriousness. This is why they are chosen as the breaker of the ranks of the common resolve. But one must be careful not to lump everyone together, for there are those who purely were ganged on because of their sheer innocence and ignorance.

CHAPTER 16

The "Sins" of Bill Clinton

If there is any American of the Anglo-Saxon descent that personified the ultimate American dream, it is Bill Clinton or officially William Jefferson Clinton. He was born to blue-collar parents who had to cope with the pressures of survival and existence. His father was an alcoholic and wife abuser while his mother was a nurse of tremendous strength of character and independence. Yet Bill Clinton dared to dream, and worse, he carried the dream to reality despite all the odds which would have limited an otherwise hapless soul.

He never served in the U.S. Army, Navy or Air Force. He even protested the Vietnam War with open marches. As if these were not enough obstacles, he came from Arkansas, a southern state with no distinct accomplishments to parade to the rest of the United States. Yet he beat the odds. He dared to put Arkansas on the billboard. More than any previous governor of that southern state, he turned around the educational fortune and with gusto, together with the business life of the state.

If the putting of Rev. Dr. Martin Luther King, Jr.'s picture in the governor's office in the southern state of Georgia by Jimmy Carter was noteworthy, the fraternization of Bill Clinton with the black people and his embrace of their equality as Americans is phenomenal. More "pungent" are his embraces of their ideas and their worthiness to serve and make America stronger in any capacity they choose, not in form of tokenism but in profound acceptance that every American is born equal. These are deadly "sins" as far as the conservative Anglo-Saxons are concerned, never mind the political party labels.

The right wing political machines swung into action one more time, having failed to stop his election as the president of the United States. They were hell bent to make his presidency an embarrassment to the United States of America by any means necessary. The first order of business was to appoint an independent prosecutor recommended by the Republican majority in the House of Representatives to the attorney general and confirmed by the three appellate court judges previously appointed by a Republican administration. From then on, every way was being sought to pounce on this unsuspecting and friendly guy who happens to be an Anglo-Saxon, very unusual.

David Karash, a cult figure of the religious right, held his followers, including women and children, hostage for so many days with stockpile of arms and ammunitions. Karash dared the law enforcement agents who suspected him of drug involvement to come into his Waco compound and arrest him. Rather than being taken alive, David Karash set the compound on fire with explosives and gasoline, two deadly ingredients, killing everyone who had not escaped. Foul was proclaimed by the Republican congress, and they quickly set congressional hearing to admonish the president. They were angrier when the attorney general, Janet Reno, took responsibility for the action taken by the ATF and FBI agents. They ridiculed and accused the president of using the attorney general for cover. This was the insulting cry from these unrepentant right wingers.

One of the people assigned to dig up dirt on Bill Clinton found that he and his wife, Hilary, had a land deal twenty years ago involving the Savings and Loans Bank. They quickly summoned the independent prosecutor, a card-carrying Republican noted for dirty mudslinging and smearing, to follow the smell of the Whitewater land deal in Arkansas sixteen years before Clinton became the president of the United States and found him guilty by association. From then on, it was a field day for anyone, especially women, who would like to be famous by accusing Bill Clinton from sexual harassment to outright exposé of having had sex with him. Paula Jones, Jennifer Flowers, and other women appeared and grabbed the media headlines! They claimed to have resisted advances they once accepted. The Republican judges of the Appellate Circuit and those of the Supreme Court of the United States made the circus complete, compelling the president of the United States to give a deposition in the Whitewater investigation, in the Paula Jones sexual harassment lawsuit, etc. And some of the right wing elements even volunteered to pay the legal costs and plastic surgical cosmetic reconstruction of Paula Jones's nose and teeth to make her more appealing and consequently credible. What a spindle of web weaved! Well, Bill Clinton did not help his own case. He had to be virile and straight and appealing to women who would readily exploit his weakness. The Republicans, who only engage in partisan politics as long as they live, never lost an opportunity to embarrass a Democratic Party president. With the help of Linda Tripp, a Republican operative, they set Clinton up with a young intern, Monica Lewinsky. Monica Lewinsky, a starry-eyed, ambitious, and a willing tool to advance a fantasy, was readily available with no brain to match.

With a needy Clinton at vulnerable moments, Monica would appear ever ready to seduce. Clinton fell into the trap, and the rest of the story is a footnote of history, and what a footnote! Having failed to derail a Clinton presidency including the shutting down of the federal government functions through the Republican right wing putsch, Clinton's enemies found a ready culpable weapon for Kenneth Starr who had been promised a plum senatorial nomination for the Commonwealth of Virginia, having failed to get the nod for the Supreme Court seat from George Bush.

Now that Bill Clinton, through an act of indiscretion and need to satisfy his natural lust, failed to see the machination of the Republican detractors, he handed them a reason to hack down on his presidency once and for all. Everyone would then poke fun at him at every turn and, despite his achievements, would make mincemeat of his presidency. What a shame! Every impotent and discredited politician became a puritan.

For a president who had sustained the longest economic growth and stability in the history of USA without any massive war abroad combined with the lowest unemployment statistics and social peace at home to go down in history on account of a sexual misconduct with a common "whore" used as a bait is unfortunate indeed. But life is sometimes a boomerang, and indeed, life works in a cycle. But that cycle has to be natural and not forced. The Republican Party members would want to force that cycle by bringing charges on Clinton's presidency like the much-desired impeachment proceedings of Richard M. Nixon, the last Republican Party president who deserved the disgrace of being forced out of office. The lives destroyed by Richard M. Nixon while in office, if nothing else, should get him removed. This was in addition to the hate and racist inclinations and calculated so-called foreign policies––of treating Africa with benign neglect and raising the ante against the third world people. These are people needing help but who were further pushed down the abyss of economic devastation.

CHAPTER 17

Everyone Is Enjoying the Benefits of Clinton's Presidency

Whoever wrote about the epicurean indulgence must have had the foresight of describing a new people called the present-day Americans. Yes, with opulence and devil-may-care attitudes, they indulge. But thanks to the few, whatever their motives, who remind the Americans that there's a world out there and larger than theirs, a world where what affects it would ultimately affect the continental nation of the USA. But without the few to bring reality home to America in different ways, the brainwashing and complete shutdown of the senses would have been completed.

The moneymakers would rather opt for the shutdown of the senses, for in that way, they could get the people down the epicurean path and get them to indulge while they laugh all the way to the bank. And life, despite its inequities, would never be questioned to any appreciable extent by the masses.

In this Clinton era, everyone is enjoying the economic benefit of the presidency. The natural energy of the nation was released to advance the cause of a great people who love to create for the comfort of their beings. Life continues on a social path, and people could be seen in their ordinariness without any unnecessary pomp and pageantry. This period revisits and restores the artistic past of the United States. For the first time in the nation's history, thanks to Bill Clinton, the nation is loudly and constantly talking about education, scientific advances, and the relevance of education of the modern day in the next millennium. The nation is refocusing its attention on its domestic infrastructures and how to perfect it's various institutions, which had broken down while building or laying the foundation (albeit with resistance from conservative or racist Republican Party members and supremacist groups) for a new social order of cooperation among the races. Bill Clinton has led the way that a president of the United States of America can be truly presidential in showing love, respect, and acknowledgement for all the people of America without any hidden agenda to suppress any group of people for the exclusive domination of the other.

The American people, in spite of it all, are a sensitive people. They watch the body language of their president, in their reactions to one another, and in their business dealings with each other. They read Ronald Reagan correctly for his arrogance in Americanism, and the racists followed his lead of benign neglect of the other minorities however imperfectly. They also saw through George Bush and Richard Nixon in the same vein. So they (the American people) saw Clinton's "sins' as having nothing to do with his performance as a president. In fact, opinion polls after another saw no severity of the effect of sexual behavior orchestrated or planned to entrap a sitting president of the United States of America. The people as well as the senate trying to dethrone the president saw a right wing puritanical plot at work. The impeachment therefore failed.

Finally, this is the first time--a lot of people might say it was long coming--that the average citizen is interested in the stock markets. The surge and splurge have been phenomenal to say the least from the Northeast to the deep South and Western states. All innuendoes for catastrophe to mar this era have been rendered to naught.

From the same judges and congressmen of the Republican Party persuasions who sit in judgment of Bill Clinton to the average working man and woman, all are enjoying the benefits of Bill Clinton's presidency. If anything, the present-day Republican Party members and leadership makes it easier to understand the commitment of white or Caucasian Americans to racism or white supremacy cloaked in the guise of "thoughtful" men and women of "integrity." Even the election of the lonely American Congressman Watts in their midst makes it crystal clear what their opinion of an African American is, i.e., make a token of them to fool the larger majority of the people.

CHAPTER 18

The Fallibility of the American Power

Don't tell the average person born in the USA that his country's military power is limited because he never knew it until Vietnam. The naked use of raw power had always been America's hallmark of greatness, for example the seizure of the Indian lands, the annexing of the Mexican land through Texas, New Mexico, California, Arizona to name a few. Oversea annexation of Hawaii was in order. So was the heavy stick wielded by T. R. (Theodore Roosevelt) over the rest of South America against the Spaniards and the Portuguese. So it had been and so does the conservative-minded born-in-the-USA Caucasians think it ought to continue.

Perhaps the most naked use of American raw power was first put to action by President Harry S. Truman without due consideration for the affected people just because they were non- Europeans. I am speaking of the dropping of the atomic or nuclear bomb on Hiroshima and Nagasaki. Japan was forced to capitulate. The continuous naked show of power continued under President Kennedy who forcibly occupied Guantanamo Bay, a Cuban territory. It didn't take long for every American president to find a foreign war of aggression appealing and a way to shore up their falling domestic approval rating of their job performance. The American presidents from Johnson to Nixon to Ford remember the Mayaguez incident off the coast of the Southeast Asia.

The series of defeats since Vietnam debacle had a chilling effect for sure. Carter and Reagan wanted to revisit the commando days. In Iran and Lebanon respectively, they were greeted by rude shocks. And when Bush tried his hand in Somalia, it was badly bitten. Ever since, caution had replaced adventurism. The people of the USA now know the limits of the American power. They also know that most of the presidents use the foreign adventures to shore up their lagging domestic image or as diversions from their failing domestic agenda. Coalition with other nations became the norm in making foreign wars.

Of all the American presidents who had waged foreign wars, only Bill Clinton ever did so out of genuine interest of the American people or out of the principle of humanity. Others have done it for some financial economic gains, but only William Jefferson Clinton would prefer to limit the number of lives lost in such combat to the consternation of Republican Party members who believe that for the economy in the USA to improve, you must engage in war. George Bush failed in his bid. Despite the killings made in Panama in the name of the war on drugs and Iraq over Kuwait, the highest opinion poll rating in history, with the hoopla, did not translate to a booming economy. Instead, the economy went into a tailspin and went into a recession. George Bush benefited handsomely from the adventures, but the American people lost immensely.

Only Bill Clinton had managed so far to maintain domestic economic prosperity without a foreign war involving American ground forces abroad. He is able to do so by employing the highest common sense ever possessed by a U.S. president. Even in the face of stiff and unreasonable opposition both from the Democratic constituent and direct opposition of the Republican "congress" leadership, Bill Clinton knew how to rule and harness the best from the people. Others may view some compromises he made as weakness, but hindsight would later find these compromises as his strength. Here was a country which had had to endure a whole twelve-year move to the right. It takes a maverick like Bill Clinton to bring the country to its middle-of-the-road senses.

Bill Clinton knew there was a lot of gray in the answers to world and domestic American problems. Nudging and careful execution of options are what solves problems. Some people have mistaken rigidity for strong character and unreasonable posturing for strength. Even with a Democratic majority of representatives in the first two years of his presidency, the Southerners voted with the Republicans right in the house.

With that stroke of genius and connection with the people of the United States, the economy waxed stronger, and with the right international cooperation, the economy progressed against the slower rate of European and the recession in the Japanese economy.

The lip service paid to equality and service of races under God by other presidents from the founding fathers to Jimmy Carter and Reagan to George Bush is only practicalized by Bill Clinton. Hence the rumple and grumbling of the white supremacists during his tenure. For the first time in the life of the republic, the whites and the white wannabes were getting it that the myth of their superiority is just a myth. Clinton was the only president who, despite some people's misgivings, really went to berth for the common people who had been indexed out of the economic system. Those are "grievous sins" to the conservatives and conservatives wannabes.

From all his handling of both domestic and foreign problems, he relied on the power of persuasion and reasonable balance. Force had been used as a last resort where preservation of human life was at stake. He would not look the other way then even if nudged to do so by some know-it-all, men of military expertise as in Yugoslavia and Ireland. George Bush was not wholesomely happy for the turn of events in South Africa. I cannot recall a meeting he held with Nelson Mandela with a photo op. If George Bush is respected in America despite his callousness, then the diagnosis of the people is right on target. The Republicans are repaying him with his son's "coronation."

The universal health coverage proposed by Bill Clinton faced so much opposition from a coalition of health-insurance lobbyists and their cohorts in the U.S. Congress that the president was forced to withdraw the proposal. The opposition was built because of the fact that poor people across the United States will be covered as well as the so-called hardworking middle class and upper middle class. I'll bet anything that the situation will be revisited when the middle class and the upper counterparts find health insurance as it is unaffordable. Hatred borne out of stupidity stands to rob America of her preeminence in the world.

Everyone wants Bill Clinton to be grateful to him or her for serving the administration. How about they being grateful to Clinton for their being picked and put in the limelight? No one cares how and what pressure Clinton went through each day to make the rest of the people happy. All that mattered to the opposition and the far right hypocritical Christians was to make him pay for doing all the right things and getting them through. If he tried to alleviate the suffering of the poor, it was too late in coming, or the opposition said, or that the effort would not have worked or too little to work. If the effort was too massive, it would be another case of wasting of good resources. And when it works, they would have amnesia as to who started the process.

Finally, recognizing for the first time in the history of the nation that wrongs have been inflicted on the third-world nations, particularly in Africa and South America, through a policy of racism embedded into the fabric of bureaucratic operations, I think Bill Clinton could take solace in his accomplishments by the relief of debts piled on the poor citizens through the connivance of their "leaders" with the racist lender nations.

Nothing exposed the behavior of the dominant Caucasian in America like the event of the 2001 and after the American government played on the fear and continues to do so of the majority and drives home the insecurity of the immigrant and the "lesser" than Caucasian yellow race or white-wannabe Arabs, Christians, or Muslims of the Middle East. This is a great country with those at the helms of affairs behaving like little village heads suffering from xenophobia. For starters, the body language of an American president must be measured so as not to be misinterpreted by the rest of the "lesser" world. So also are his public utterances were not provoked or necessitated for policy affirmation. The critique is not out of malice or prejudice, but with a view to point out to an otherwise complacent society too quick to judge and ascribe blame to other "lesser" beings to their vulnerabilities, that it is less than perfect after all. In fact, the society is as ordinary as the other creatures of God. I am as sure as pure diamond that this observation is well documented and known by the subjects but they are too afraid or egotistical to admit their ordinariness. For whatever it's worth, human hands are too short to box with God.

It is one thing to be distraught with the catastrophic events of September 11, 2001, but it is another not to admit the culpability in abetting the situations howbeit inadvertently. Learning from the mistakes that led to that event while pursuing its perpetrators could have been managed differently if counsel had been taken from all Americans instead of frontal confrontations with the entire world and squandering the resources of America in a war that was going nowhere. All it had done is get us paranoid about our state of being. Then again, America, especially the "dominant" group, loves this state drama, which gives impression of hard work as opposed to steady tranquility that may be interpreted as boring no matter the accomplishment.

The event of September 11, 2001 still leaves me flabbergasted that a group of supposed leaders of a great edifice called America would allow such a catastrophe to occur on their watch and later resorting to witch hunting of the "lesser" and other hopeless beings and ruining the economy that was so delicately brought back to life. This great nation must demonstrate that she cannot be dragged down by the low lives of the world that may have felt the actions the United States government impacted on the situation of their lives. Right or wrong, their concern must be addressed and correctly so for America to regain her preeminence as during the Clinton years.

The Jewish think-tank, which includes the elected politicians, the Jewish members of the media, and the plain Jewish ethnic person, would vote for and agree with any administration in America fighting one way or another to preserve the Jewish state whether such administration merits it or not or just using such diversion to preserve a strangle hold on power. Many White Anglo Saxon Protestants, not wise to the Anglo name change of the Jewish American individuals and because of the Anglo name recognition, would echo the same sentiment in solidarity only to be betrayed in the "deepest consequence." But because of the fear of looking stupid, the argument would be advanced even if wrongheaded. The ego of personal frame of reference is still at play. I have no illusion that this observation would not be attacked and riddled with bombastic expression of vilifications by the truly affected because of its deadly accuracy.

Now that the Supreme Court of the United States has struck down the pretentious sodomy law in Texas with reverberations across the land, we can expect a floodgate of expressions throughout the country. Very soon, gays or homosexuals can expect to kiss openly on night and day television programs in the citizen's living rooms. Soon would follow the leadership of the churches and finally acquiescence and acceptance with open arms as if nothing was ever the case. One would only hope that acceptance of fundamental human rights of non-Caucasians without any qualms and blushing and castigations would be the order of the day. Everyone today knows that without the so-called affirmative actions, the better qualified nonwhite candidate, in fact, the black or African racial groups, would be deliberately kept out of reach of education and promotion on the jobs they've mastered so well. Sometimes, a qualified Caucasian has been victimized deliberately to skew the debate in order to claim a reverse discrimination or racism to make nonsense of the fight for equality. Now, that homosexuality has been recognized in today's world, it must be addressed headlong and settled. There is so much on settling issue in this admission. Life has been throwing humanity these curve balls for some years now.

Theories abound about the why and how the gay lifestyle rises to this unmanageable stage. Among the "lesser" world of African philosophy, it is believed that something happened during the pregnancy when the mother had a walk one afternoon or the dead of night while alien spirit roamed the face of the planets. During this time, manipulation by the spirits in the changing of the fetus inside the mother in terms of personality would occur, resulting in atypical beings of the extraterrestrial that roam the earth as humans and otherwise, but we won't go there! There has to be a scientific explanation to all this and such is the following. There is a theory that the first trimester of pregnancy in female humans is attended with rapid cell divisions of multiple cell lines with great dynamism of the HLA genetic code. The HLA-D region has the greatest dynamism. This region could result in the bizarre or normal phenotypic picture of the human person. It is at this stage that abnormality of any type could occur, be it deformity of any of the vital organs. Timely recall of genetic switch of the organs is hereby sealed. Now, what happens here may be affected by gene modulation, obliteration, or atrophy, which may be the result in different humans with varying behavioral patterns. Since the androgens and other hormonal factors responsible for the whole genetic makeup and gender differences with attending feelings there have been established, all bets are off on the finished products.

The rise again of the American power rests on her ability to move to champion the creed of our Constitution and truly move to lead the world with the content of our moral rectitude. After all, to the boss who hired efficient and productive lieutenants go the glory of the era. He will be discovered to be smarter than the lieutenants with the mile-long paper trail of qualifications. I never for once discounted good academic qualifications, but I hasten to add that with no additional human attribute, it will amount to little in the global context.

Diplomacy with genuine realization of facts will win America more friends, thereby protecting this long-suffering experiment of ideas called democracy. Exploration and consideration scientific, medical, and artistic of ideas from all the immigrants that makeup the American nation devoid of unnecessary manipulation for "ass kissing" would eventually save the nation.

CHAPTER 19

The Parental Responsibility and Child Upbringing

Few people will argue the facts, but most people born in the USA would never accept the responsibility of their failure as parents both as conservatives and the much celebrated liberals. There's much to say for children bearing children, especially children who had not accepted good home training. Who would learn from whom? It is a case of the blind leading the blind. One could say that disobedience to parental authority is a culture of those born in the USA, which they are exporting to the rest of the world via the media and video and movies. Unfortunately, the children of those poor countries are vulnerable to these kinds of garbage. They suck it up and never get better since then. This actually provides cover for the USA that the world is after all in their mold.

Violence incite violence. When one American advises the other, the room to sneer becomes multiple. Racism and strong belief in racism came from half-baked adults who grow to be old with the brainwashed ideas they possessed before they had their children. You just have to listen to the hot air coming from the mouth of some of the Southern members of the U.S. Congress and the so-called Midwestern cracker or redneck states. Any wonder that the problems of racism become so intractable for such a strong nation.

Ever since childhood, self-gratification and indulgence have been the norm of those born in the USA. From the beginning of times, the efforts of a few well-meaning adult parents are often negated by the system. For one, the system would deprive the new non-English speaking immigrants of the chance to raise the newborn in the USA with the values of the old world. Yes, some of those old values are flawed, but they can be corrected or modified. To compound the situation, we have adolescent psychologists who never had children of their own and never knew what it takes to raise children telling everyone else, social workers included, how to raise their children. It is a case of book psychologist! Unending gratification and reinforcements for good behavior, however slight, without reprimands for bad ones is the method of these so-called professionals. The only times the people get reprimanded would be after they have committed some gruesome crimes and put in the prison system. This was how life was carried on and this is how it's been pursued with minor adjustments to favor a few choice individuals. And these are the born-in-the-USA *Mayflower* descendants.

The crust of the problem is that while the government of the USA would want to keep the citizens ignorant, little do the lawmakers know that their actions would eventually come back to haunt them. The world works like a boomerang. It is often stated but not wholesomely believed that what goes up must come down. The world is round, and boomerang is the law of nature whether one believes it or not. Had man the necessary intelligence, insidious actions would have been refrained from. They would have known that the slave trade action would haunt them for life. And children of innocent new non-English speaking immigrants from Italy and east Europe and Portugal would grow to destroy the edifices the early Anglo-Saxon immigrants built.

Nature compensates and handsomely too! The reverberations have been low birth rates for Anglo-Saxons. And when they deliberately wish to increase such population growth, they are rewarded with delinquent and problematic offspring with questionable contributive abilities to the society. Even with that, they (Anglo-Saxons) want the rest of the oppressed humans to rally round their problems and show more-than-normal compassion which they would ordinarily not show to the offspring of the oppressed with similar difficulties.

But there are rays of hope. Starting from Bill Clinton, there have been individuals within the Caucasian ranks showing signs of humanity and understanding that they are not superior in anyway over other human beings. The point of this topic is that the lack of the ability to be good parents still haunts the born-in-the-USA Caucasians and those who have been unfortunate to come under their tutelage or brainwashing instructions and grew with it.

Therefore, except for the trouble that has been introduced in the third world, i.e., the dividing of the people against themselves, thereby losing focus of their mission, the person born in the USA has nothing to teach the third-world immigrants on the upbringing of children and loving them.

CHAPTER 20

The Media as Instrument of Confusion

Most modern nations would welcome the information media as the eyes and ears of the general public. But most governments of nations have often used the information media as their instruments of confusion for the people they govern. Western nations have started to use the media more efficiently before the communists came to latch on to it howbeit imperfectly. The dawn of perfect use of the media reached its height with Germany's Adolf Hitler. But before him was Britain and the American media houses. More was invested in the propagation of self- indulging information. Propaganda often enabled the Western nations to rally the people for wars. The people are rallied by the people in power against people deemed enemies of the state. The media made the demonization of such individuals and made it easy for the final state onslaught. Bribery, calumny, and deception and false information have been fed to the people to help their confusion further. Usually if the cases had involved other born-in-the-USA Caucasians and reversed, showing errors in the judgment before the launching of such vendetta, the people become wiser. When the victims are non-Caucasian and/or African American or African immigrants, the cases of atrocities committed against them are never recounted or regretted.

Blatant cases in point involve atrocities committed against the American Indians, the Cherokee people, and the Africans brought to slavery against their will. The media want to perpetuate absence of guilt from the perpetrators and the victim to bear the fault of the crime.

Movies and false illustrations of mindless massacre of the "good and peace-loving" Caucasians by Cherokee Indians or African slaves filled the air to justify the annihilation of the people.

For many years, the media had fed the people with illusion of superiority of the Caucasian settlers based on their race only to start taking back the false information after the premises of their campaign have been shown to be flawed. What other insults would be heaped on a maligned people than to accuse their own people of selling them to slavery or selling their lands for liquor as in the grabbing of Indians' land. As if there had not been Caucasian slaves before! The word *slave* came from *slavic* of the East Europe. Does this make right the sins of a few people even if true to be visited on a population? It should not and cannot be condoned.

CHAPTER 21

On Education

For many years, the average born-in-the-USA citizen has been brainwashed to believe that the nation's education is second to none just as they believe that their country is the strongest superpower. A thoughtful few has told the masses that while the nation is mighty in war arsenal and latest technologies, the future generations would have to depend on immigrants just arriving from Europe, Russia, and Africa even if they whispered the last continent. The blanks have not been completed without the inclusion of Asia. After all, the much-heralded computer age was invented by an Asian immigrant, an Indian young mathematician. The conjectures and the configuration were in place before Bill Gates and Jobs got to capitalize on it.

The truth of the matter is that the United States was never started or created as a "brainiard" nation. The creation was from the seizure of lands, which belongs to the Indians the English met here. The expansion was possible by seizure of lands belonging to the Mexicans and other Miskito Indians of the South and in the Pacific region. The American businessmen need no lesson on how to make use of cheap labor.

Earlier, we discussed the American method of child upbringing that literally would be the litmus test for the development of interest in education. Practical superficial education has been very abundant in the USA from the dawn of time. While the basis and premises for good education is present, most born-in-the-USA citizens never take advantage of it because of the discipline involved. The field of good education is often left for the new immigrant and their young children as a condition for recognition and citizenship. It may not have been verbalized or entered into the law books, but new immigrants and their children are often held to a higher standard of discipline and hard life than the born-in-the-USA citizens. African immigrants are obviously held to more for every cent they earn in this "land of the free."

Despite the odds of a new country culture clashing with the cultures they grew up with before coming to the USA, immigrants are expected to perform better than those born in the USA in every educational and endurance huddle while holding down jobs to sustain themselves and their families if they have any. Only in the last five to six years has education been given the hard look it deserves and the federal government, especially the executive branch, making it easier for the citizens and legal immigrants to acquire the necessary education without greater financial burden. But the facts remain that the background of the student is necessary for prediction for success with the necessary education.

Yes, America today seems to love education, but that's second to brigandage and rough-shod racist play against people of color and black immigrants. "White" America would applaud the rough and the uncouth behavior among them before they would, the proper-mannered ones. I will never understand that for a people that always cry about the rule of law. When that law is applied to them, then the law is unfair. We have observed the cowboy persona of Ronald Reagan when he was president of the United States of America. The religious right and other right wing conservatives are longing for the return of Ronald Reagan's earlier years in the White House.

The love of education and emphasis placed on education has always been a lip service before President Clinton. Service and blue-collar types of job are the hallmarks of the nation. The majority of entrepreneurs in the United States is mainly people with little formal education. The maintenance of the creativity is left for the children of recent European and Jewish immigrants anxious to climb into the American mainstream through education before their own children fall into the malaise like the generations before them. To cover the tracks of those born in the

USA, the system quickly approves the application for citizenships for European immigrants.

When the American children are compared with the Europeans and Japanese, the Americans always score lower. The educationists in America always think that the only way to even the score is to laden the children with more work without breaks, thereby driving the children to hate the education they are supposed to love and desire. We have again come back to the frail ego problem. It would have been nice if the experts in the USA really take the methods of these European countries into consideration before fashioning American designs. But no, America is supposed to be second to none, meaning that these experts would learn from no one else. Also, as long as the survey could be doctored to show that white kids are doing better than black kids, they (the "experts") feel their work is done. As long as material possession is rated higher than educational knowledge acquisition, U.S. education would continue to go south or experience nose dives. Emphasis of material possession should be downplayed in the lives of parents and children relationship. Education for the sole reason of acquisition of money should be deemphasized. Other incentives should be given for educational attainments.

Finally, the education of the American children would require a complete face-lift from the psychological repair of the mentors (education experts) to the parents of the children being cared for. The stress factor of the parents must be reduced substantially from the standpoint of job security and performance of the job in terms of volume––quota system. The children must be given breathing spaces in their schools with more social interaction promoted among the races by the responsible teachers, thereby lessening racial tensions which some children may have brought with them from their respective homes.

Also, schools or authorities of the respective schools must try to acknowledge and accommodate constructive criticisms and inputs from well-meaning parents irrespective of the accents in speaking and racial groups from which those constructive viewpoints come. Pseudo-psychological diagnosis of anomaly that is not present in children must be vigorously discouraged. Diagnosis of ailments and fitting of ailments into parameters not clearly spelt out just in order for the "experts" or professionals to earn a living must be stopped forthwith. Treatment of children as if they are adults no matter their ability to articulate their sophomoric concerns should be stopped in order to unclog the wheels of educational progress.

Parents looking for special *Mayflower* treatment of their children should be asked to transfer their children to England where they would meet their match. Pushing children up grade levels without merit must be stopped while other encouragement to learning found or devised. The government must continue to supervise parochial institutions for conformity with national school curriculum. For safety against the return of armed violence in the schools, the authorities of the cities and states must ignore the cry of the ACLU on irresponsible granting of rights.

Meanwhile, parents of Caucasian children must stop making inciting statements of bigotry to their children and stop hoping the children would not act on those statements. They must stop taking out their frustrations of economic pressures on already-disadvantaged minority groups or perceived successful minority groups just because they (Caucasians) do not like the non- Caucasian faces or skins.

One can empathize with the everyday pressures of life in the USA. No one feels these more than the minority citizens and the African and other new immigrants trying to cope with everyday existence and not the luxury which is giving the Caucasian the "hickes."

With pent-up dissatisfactions while the white bosses rake up the lion shares of the benefits generated by the labors of the minority and nonwhites, the Caucasians would eventually set themselves up for destruction. There are signs of such destruction showing up in the symptoms for devastating physiological diseases and mental health instability both in the young and old of their population.

Finally, teachers, for fear of repeating myself, must stop giving undue advantage to average Caucasian children for fear of being mislabeled. Children must be judged fairly. Efforts to destroy the lives of the minority or African American male children through their school record must be discouraged and stopped forthwith. Actions of this nature come back to haunt. They (actions) may manifest in the destruction of the children they are trying to preserve.

CHAPTER 22

Common Pattern of Resistance to Progressive Initiatives

For a moment, you would be flabbergasted that the Americans never learned and that without a deep thought of a proposition would be led by different private companies, which only consider its own interest in opposing any progressive initiative by any progressive-minded president of the nation. I have yet to witness the kind of rabid opposition to any dumb initiative which would cost the economic folding of the families, proposed often by the conservative-leaning president of the United States. Several examples abound but I will site a few.

When George W. Bush (2001–2008), in the midst of a senseless untaxed war in Iraq, proposed a four-hundred-dollar giveaway to every taxpayer with or without merit, there was not a whimper from the so-called "economic minded" and US-deficit hawks of the conservative members of the U.S. Congress and their benefactors in the private sectors. With the sleight of hand, the two groups sailed through by blackmailing the liberal members of the congress to silence since, should they protest the giveaway, they would be labeled hypocrites for daring to deny the poor the much-needed stipends to augment their meager incomes. After all, the liberals were the ones often crying foul against the conservatives' harsher disregard for the poor, after labeling them as too dependent on the government. With the declaration of war in Iraq, which had nothing to do with the 9/11 terrorist disaster and the concoction of the presence of nuclear war machine development and labeling anyone who dared to oppose the war, a nonpatriot, all of us had been gagged!

The same tactics were employed against the poor and the United States economy by Ronald Reagan (1980–1988). With the meager sum being given to disoriented, assaulted poor by conservative social media scapegoat desire, the food stamps and much of the economic safety net provisions were sharply cut or reduced with nothing else to cushion the effects as incentives to be less dependent on government. No one spoke against these draconian policies from the Christian church-going, Caucasian members of the conservative congress and their business leader cohorts. Ronald Reagan went out a hero of right wing politics, but invariably dealt with by karma, if you will. I know here in the United States you must not mention the law of retributive justice against a conservative hero! But speak; we must to unburden our conscience, if you will!

But let us examine the events that took place when President Barack Obama proposed the Affordable Health Care Act in response to the skyrocketing cost of healthcare maintenance and its looming explosion on the U.S. budget in years to come! Hell hath no fury as a woman scorned! Every lie and misinformation and calamities that would befall the United States should the ACA be enacted was predicted by the pseudo experts and pretenders to raw intelligence of the conservative realm. This was the first occasion that revealed the masters of these false professors of economics and politics. The health insurance companies, aided by the drug company cartels fearing the lowering of their income from sales of their toxic drugs by more streamlined monitoring of the prescriptions, went to war against the Affordable Care Act.

The writers and the supposedly intended beneficiaries—viz., the sick and old, uneducated Caucasians of the deep South and the rural West and Midwest—were paid and misinformed about the intention of the ACA. They were provided with written placards and buses to journey to the nation's capital to register their discontent and concern with rude and racist overtones against the occupants of the White House. Soon after, the Tea Party political organization, named after the popular uprising against the British monarchy's rule, was formed and with several million dollars in aid to topple the newly won Democratic party-led Congress. The Democrats barely survived to hold on to the Senate from then on. A series of initiatives were obstructed by these misfits whose masks of several years were finally taken off to reveal their true characters. Even in defeats, they would want to prove that they were loyal obstructionist servants of big business against their fellow citizens.

When Ronald Reagan (1980–1988) proposed to bloat the military and defense budgets which were never necessitated, everyone but a few signed on, sensing benefits financially for them through the army and defense business contractors for the plum government largess. The bloating, to this day, has not been tamed. The Republican members of Congress often would say they act "in the interest of the American people." What they mean by that can only be understood within the context of their party's code, mostly in the negative with the rest of the nation. And yet they try to want the people to view them as fiscally responsible. Too bad the liberal Democrats often remain silent either because they are shy of fighting for the poor or afraid of being labeled fighters of class war or afraid for their own internal scandals to be made public.

George W. Bush's (2000–2008) tax refunds amidst the war in Iraq left the office with the worst budget deficit and in its trail allowed China to hold America hostage on its government bond purchase amounting to trillions of dollars. Again, nothing has been whispered on this and a conspiracy or forgetfulness reigns in the Congress of the United States only to be replaced by the loudest drums of war ever beaten against meager entitlement programs, social security benefits, Medicare and Medicaid, and other college education programs.

This behavior is not new. Witness the vilification of FDR when social security, Medicare, Medicaid was proposed for the general citizenry. The hard-core racists, modern-day Republican members of congress have not sheathed their swords. They cry all along that the poor must be neglected and, at worst, made poorer. Unfortunately, the poor population is yet to find a continuous financially successful defender of their plights. Poor President Obama, he is left on his own to defend the poor in the face of barrage of opposition and various schemes to sabotage his signature health care act for the general population.

Even the Democrats from the impoverished states in the Southern and Midwestern parts of the country are threatening to oppose the health care act instead of voicing how to fix it and make it better for the poor to register for it.

This has always been the success stories of every one of the acts of Congress benefitting the poor in the United States of America. If you still doubt what I am pointing out, let us consider gun control initiatives. Measures considered to make people safe have been defeated every time it came up in the United States Congress by the gun lobby because of their own riches from gun sales defeating such initiatives. And when mentally challenged individuals, because of their inabilities to cope with the stress created by the media and environment, would end their individual turmoil, they would take with themselves several better able-to-cope citizens and children who never even started a meaningful life yet along with themselves. And what does the churchgoing members of the National Rifle Association say? "It's the people that kill. Guns do not." They offer empty condolences to those who had lost their loved ones in their milieu only to oppose any measure that would limit the loss of lives.

Unfortunately, the families of the victims of each disaster episodes, because of government inaction without moments of reflection, become latent recruits of the NRA and would join the frenzy of purchase of guns and ammunition for another round of mayhem. It is now difficult to assess the mental state of the average citizen in the area of mental stability and rationality irrespective of job acquisition, educational attainment, and position entrusted. Capability of violence must be the first consideration. No one can lecture anyone in the other parts of the world, least of all an American, about peace and Christianity or belief in God and Jesus Christ. None of the tenets of Christ's teachings has ever been imbibed in the everyday conduct of business. The old adage is forever as true now—— "to have peace, prepare for war."

Somewhere in some Southern states computer age or cyber age geeks would be assembled and paid by fat cat arch-conservative Republicans to thwart every effort for the Affordable Care Act by making the website unworkable. The nation's defense department must follow the smell of the money from the old disgruntled conservatives, drug companies, and health insurance magnates. For some reason none other than money, they would want the Affordable Care Act passed into law to suffer the same fate like the Clinton's stillborn efforts of 1990s.

CHAPTER 23

Ethnic Politics in the United States

I used to condemn the ethnic politics of the people of the third world and Africa. In particular, I believed that in the United States, the politics of ethnic preference would not stand, that every American would be treated equally before the law of the land. Boy was I wrong! It did not take long for me to realize the fool's paradise I had created in my mind out of ignorance––of the premises fictitiously written in the United States Constitution.

Apart from the desire to serve in every capacity of this country and the payments of taxes required to maintain the social infrastructure of the environment and the edifices of government from the work or job one engages in, what one gets back in terms of return for services rendered is based on your ethnicity and connections to the powers that be. In such cases, you are either a tool to be used to mask the true machinations of the promoters or a hapless citizen set up for failure when the ovation is highest and sent crumbling or crashing to the very ground, never to reach that height again.

Now, this ethnic politics, approached diligently, is dependent on who you are and in which part of the country you are operating. And it varies from people to people. It also depends on one's own personal frame of reference and whether you share certain philosophy with certain ethnics or not before you may be accepted as a proxy member. If you are vehemently, openly critical of your own ethnic group, you stand a chance of being accepted and promoted by the higher pyramids of other ethnics as a proxy. This way, you may be set up only to be cut to size if you should forget who you are!

In the United States, at the top of the pyramids are the Anglo-Saxon Caucasians, comprising of immigrants from England, Germany, Scotland, loosely followed by the central Europeans with less clout as the upper echelon and the southern Europeans. The eastern Europeans are important as members only in the business sphere and in numbers to maintain strength of the population. The Asian population is another ethnic group divided along the following groups––in the southern part and the Pacific, the east Indian extraction, the Chinese extractions, and the Japanese stand apart. At the top of the pyramid seat, the Anglo-Saxon decides which of the lower echelons of the intelligentsia would be given figments of approval and acceptance into their club of ethnic dominance which, among the members of the ethnics at the periphery, would be used as pawns against others while they maintain tactical innocence of whatever is going on, only to sit as judge and jury deciding the fate of the erring pons.

Depending on the ambition or ignorance or both of the members of the peripheral ethnics, they may present themselves as willing pawns by playing up to the deciding Anglo-Saxons at the apex of the pyramids. Especially if one of their own is found wanting, they often would choose the flagrant play for certain period of time. Occasionally, things may not work as planned and forceful sidelining or removal of the pawn may be necessitated. It is an unwritten rule, which nevertheless is clearly obvious that the pawn must play according to the rule, which is perpetuating the domination of the population by the members of the apex council.

Now, the members of the apex know which ethnic group would be bad choices for pawns, and often their growth in rank is often clipped. Because of such ethnic hegemony and sulking disposition for not being considered for the ruling membership, the rise is limited, and such action may even be applauded by other lower ethnic groups because of display of arrogance and disrespectful behaviors to the others. Bad conduct or injustices done to some other ethnic groups in the past may rule them out of consideration for longer-term pawn use for fear of those members seeking vengeance or redress for those offenses by the ruling class. Women from the ruling class ethnic family are seldom allowed to reach such heights because they could be emotionally "unstable." These women who may be hardened snubs more than their men may often give in to raw emotions and pangs of conscience weakness. They may display rare aspects of human qualities. This is unacceptable within the group. Life to them is meaningless without this inhuman game of pitting on ethnic group against the other, destabilizing one and trying to capture the elite profile like their own or trying to be financially successful also. Witness London, Kentucky, USA, at the turn of the twentieth century.

Think about it, this writer may not identify the other ethnic groups too clearly, or he may become the victim of his own insight by a pawn from his own ethnic background. Such is the situation in the USA, sometimes like the rest of the world, which is hardly criticized by the elite ethnics here for such behavior they are heavily guilty of.

For justice, think again and survey the punishments for whatever crime received by member of lower ethnic groups and compare it with what is rendered to the ordinary Anglo-Saxon members of the group. Enough said already! Now, most of the young members of various lower and peripheral ethnic groups want to have clean slates for interactions! How far they would go remains to be seen before the idealist proposition is poisoned by the rearing of disruptive beach head of ignorant and felonious elements of the same youthful class against the laudable quest.

With President Lyndon B. Johnson, 1963–1968, it took a lot of arm twisting and browbeating and downright presidential bullying and horse trading, including blackmail, to get the Civil Rights Act passed. Today, most of the right wing conservatives who were opposed to the act would point to the enactment as the proudest moment of the United States when talking to strangers or the ignorant citizens who never knew of the parts they played in the debacle.

Most members of the committees on government and judicial and civil rights matters, having positioned themselves, are from the South, and they were dead set against granting equal human rights to all citizens of the United States, especially the African Americans. Lyndon Johnson had to work on the chairmen of these committees and their Southern rank and files before the act was allowed to be put to vote and passed.

Another obstacle would soon need to be crossed over in the busing of school children in order to achieve racial integration in the schools with the children of the United States. This also required a hell of a fight and involved the conservative members of Congress with faint support of some of the liberal northerners with "democratic credentials." I need not have to state that they were mostly Caucasians or whites, both male and female. They enlisted the members of the Caucasian and Caucasian wannabe public to oppose the integration of the school system.

One thing I have come to observe here in the United States of America is the tendency of the majority of the Caucasian or white population to engage in the derisive name calling often heaped on the victims of their wrong-headed arguments to buttress their points. Often, it is easy to talk about the breakdown of law and order without talking about how it came to be.

I write here to point to the history of the Caucasian population of the United States of mostly in opposition to measures that will include the minorities in benefits that will improve their lifestyles or economic well-beings. So for progress to be made by the United States in interacting with the rest of the world, especially the third or developing world, to trust the United States' intentions, services and transparent steps must be taken to address the inequity within her borders as it refers to the non-Caucasian and black citizens of the nation.

President Barack H. Obama has been working against the wind of reactionary opposition. Some members of cabinet even wait to see him falter only to pounce and point to his "inadequacy" in the pursuit of peace and better lives for the entire citizenry of the United States. So he has not been the only progressive president maligned and obstructed by the retrogressive conservatives; only the vituperation is louder and unrelenting even more than Clinton's with marital or financial scandal to hang on him.

The media, which pretend to be progressive often, pander to the regressive forces in order to be seen as being fair in news coverage. Many of the so-called conservative news people are on the payroll of the conservative businessmen or organizations in one disguise or the other to escape being detected. When any conservative administration do not rush to bomb out a weak third-world country, he is deemed weak in governance.

They would want to act without realizing or wanting to realize that the world dynamic is different now. Gone are the days of complete dominance with no consequences. Yet the conservative right wing elements in the United States see no changes in the world, nor would they acknowledge such even if it is brought to their doorsteps. From Arizona to the Southeast to Texas and some areas of the Midwest of the United States, these areas can boast of mostly evangelical Christian faiths, including the Episcopalian, Baptist, and other Christian denominations, yet their fair mindedness, selflessness, and human rights records can easily be called into question. Easily, they would proclaim their hypocritical "Christian" credentials.

Now, the world is realizing that the American conservatives are out of touch with reality of life. They give in to hysteria, especially based on racial discrimination against non-Caucasian minorities, notably African Americans. Their point of view on any discussion is based on racial superiority of the Caucasian which everyone knows is false and baseless. Without realizing this basis, some blacks or African Americans would be misled and fall into the misguided view of the trials of the Caucasian conservative views. Obstruction of actions to improve the economic lives of the non-Caucasian Americans is the forte of the American conservative politicians.

The American conservative politicians never cease to amaze me. They wear the label of conservative with pride, often voted for and returned to office at the federal, state, and city levels from the backward counties, cities, and states they purport to represent. Of course, they are often sure that they have beaten down their hometown electorates with brainwashing comments and condescending gestures while they laugh to the banks on the federal, state, and city salaries they coveted for themselves in the name of service.

But because of personal frame of reference, most of the electorates from these economically deprived populations would cling to their correctness in voting Republicans rather than admit to their own stupidity. Many of the districts represented by the conservative Republicans boast of backwardness, poverty, and poor educational attainments. This they turn into envy and hatred for their progressive states' compatriots. These philosophically backward areas have now been given the Bible and have self-proclaimed their righteousness and conscientious voting patterns.

You can just sum up their mentalities from their appearance of uncouthness to ill health and downright ignorance on almost everything, from education to environment and health. The devil, they say, is the driving force of the progressives while they themselves spew out the devilish aroma however financially rich or poor.

But what should be known and understood about the American psyche is that the appearance alone cannot define them just like any other human beings, and liberalism changes quite often to conservatism when the subject of discussion would affect them personally. As I have written earlier in this same book, this observation is intended to make Americans, particularly those with the Caucasian-European last names, to be aware of their behavior and utterances. This is also intended to put Americans on notice that they are being watched and measured along with their proclamation whether they live in accordance with the creed of the Constitution of the United States of America that all men and women are created equal with inalienable rights by the Almighty God.

This is unique for United States, the Constitution that is. But it is astonishing how certain elements of the citizens would interpret the Constitution in the most bizarre fashion as to favor the privileged and crime via the amendments.

The Constitution puts the United States of America in the unique position of a standard in nationhood if the practitioners live up to its creed.

CHAPTER 24

Final Diagnosis

In the end, no one can really blame those born in the USA. No one makes anyone to stay in the USA. Neither did the people of America force anyone (immigrants) to come to their country. But no one could underestimate the power of persuasion; be it through advertisement, cajoling, and extolling the virtues of USA through citizens who unwillingly became the agent provocateurs for the impression created in the minds of the immigrants. Also, economic deprivation sometimes brought about by mismanagement of the immigrants' political leaders in their home countries or a result of some unfortunate natural calamities or disasters contributed to the decisions of the immigrants to come to the USA. Many of them, having come and hopefully willing to remain for a few years, were trapped by various constraints, viz., children and economic consideration.

There is the fear that the situation of the home country would get worse economically based on the news reaching the New World. No one could underestimate the roles of the Central Intelligence Agency and other clandestine intelligence organizations in this modem time in undermining the immigrants' home national progress in order to contain the aspirations of the immigrants to return home. Recent events in Southeast Asia and all Asia nearing economic collapse gives one food for thought. Now the Asians who have been of tremendous help, along with the Africans for the boisterous American economy, must stay put in the New World. The situation is even precarious for the disorganized Africans in the USA. It is one sordid news of disaster after another, constantly fueling the insidious fear of returning to the lands of their birth and finally losing their culture or a chance to fine-tune it to be capable of modern-day emulation. One cannot say for sure, but indicators and history point to the ongoing paranoia of those born in the USA to remain at the "preeminence" of power over the rest of the world of varying shades of color. Some have said the calamities and destruction caused by human intrigues have found those born in the USA right at the center and bottom of it. But we will leave it at that while our diagnosis and observation remain the subject of debate for those who may want to disprove our assertion to cloud the truth further.

The Caucasian or look-alike Caucasian born in the USA like the twisted Oedipus complex makes sure that Europe, the ancestral land, remain viable and flourishing to the detriment of other lands while the born-in-the-USA Africans or African Americans scuttle around denying their connection with their African origins. They are ashamed because of the absence of constructive minds to put a better picture of the continent on the map. They hurry to mark their association by insisting that they have no other origin except in the USA. But intelligent minds know better.

There is even that need by many an infantile personalities to cry and try to want to have their ways at all costs. And if no one calls his or her bluffs, the recklessness would go on unabated.

Such is the psyche of those born in the USA, both white and black. Sometimes with the behavioral pattern ubiquitous in the continent, one feels compelled to assign a genetic verdict. So severe is the behavior that a new immigrant to this land may become confused by the unseemly irrationality. But one must not make a final judgment of every person born in the USA. Indeed there are some of the finest of the human species among them, perhaps shaped by the experiences of their grandparents or their own life experiences.

What really has become the cancer on the behaviors of those born in the USA is the notion that they are superior to other human beings. The behavior brought from England by their forebears became so infectious that it affected and dictated the classical and sometimes senseless reaction even of former slaves among themselves––the light-skinned slaves, often products of rapist masters, feeling superior to the dark-skinned slaves who were products of true love experiences. Whenever the light-skinned is rejected by the Caucasian born in the USA, then you see them cross over to align themselves with the dark skinned and try to champion the cause of the oppressed which he would not have joined had he not been victimized personally. Women of course remain unrepentant house negroes sometimes. Nonetheless, women of the born-in-the- USA descendants of the early slaves have managed to receive the mercies of their masters and mistresses, serving them with unflinching loyalty even or sometimes at the expense of their own race. They have either willfully or with force bore children for them. And with their wits, they have been able to create wealth for themselves by the time of the Emancipation. Women of the caliber of Harriet Truman and the like are very few exceptions. Hence, the lives of these rare breeds must be celebrated.

The resilience to bounce back with dignity and refusal to roll over and yet celebrate hope and life for the living has always been the hallmark for survival carried over from Africa in the midst of the calamities in to the New World. When you are born free, your love of freedom knows no bound. I fail to see the excuse today. Now that we are born free in the New World, African Americans must continue to celebrate that freedom and embrace their African kin who never experienced what slavery was in spite of their poverty. The barrier artificially created must be broken down mentally. Africans both from home and in the diaspora must mix it up and atrophy all the decadent genes of slavery in our somatic body cell and blood so that their strength could be wholesome and lasting as it should be.

Just as the born-in-the-USA Caucasians form a real bond with their European cousins, providing them with jobs and giving them real access to bank credits and greatness in modern- day America, so should the born-in-the-USA African descendants close rank with their kin from across the Atlantic Ocean instead of denying such glaring kinship.

The Almighty God is omniscient, omnipresent, and omnipotent. We have not been told which religion He prefers as His. There are thousands of religions to be sure. Therefore, the choice of religion by individuals in the USA cannot be official for everyone. One would have thought that the people who profess to believe in and worship the Almighty God would respect His wishes. The Creator knows His own intentions and has put all of the people on this earth together. The same people who would die for a monument of God's commandments would easily discriminate against groups of other humans created by God, judge them, and condemn them for not being created to look like themselves.

I would hope that the self-inflicting prejudice of the Caucasian would not be too infectious as to destroy the immunity of other races driving them to insanity. Sure, Asians are also discriminating, but theirs as well as the Africans' would be understood and treated with topical remedy rather than with major surgery. The Asians' prejudice, like the Caucasians in the USA and Western Europe, is based on ignorance and backwardness based on delusion of superiority. Let them get over it. They are just as ordinary as the rest of us! We will all die individually or collectively, never remembering whatever we have become in the physical state but spiritually powerful according to the goodness of our work in the previous world. Don't get me carried away now. All I say here is to let go and get off the illusionary high horses and really enjoy life.

In the end, the hidden philosophy of the Caucasians and the other infected groups of people of the USA may be about money, power, and sex––in that order. The epicurean philosophy is forever on display.

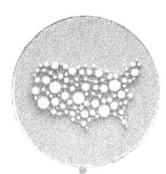

BIBLIOGRAPHY

African Americans: Voices of Triumph. Alexandria, Virginia: Time-Life Books, 1993. "The AIDS Cover-Up." *Tony Brown's Journal*, PBS Nov. 27, 1992.

"Finds Touch of Africa in 28 Million Whites." Associated Press, June 15, 1958.

Abernathy, Ralph. *And the Walls Came Troubling Down.* New York: Harper and Row Publishers, 1989.

Abdul-Jabbar, Kareem, and Alan Steinberg: Black Profiles in Courage: A Legacy of African American Achievement. New York: William Morrow and Company, 1996.

Bennett, Lerone, Jr. *Before the Mayflower: A History of Black America*, 5th ed. New York: Penguin Books, 1982.

Brown, Tony. *Black Lies, White Lies.* New York: HarperCollins, 1995.

Browne, Malcolm W. "What is Intelligence, and Who Has It?" *The New York Times Book Review*, October 16, 1994.

Comot, Robert. *A Streak of Luck.* New York: Bantow Books, 1980.

DeParle, Jason. "Talk of Government Being Out to Get Blacks falls on More Attentive Ears."

The New York Times, October 29, 1990.

Fletcher, Marvin E. *The Black Soldier and Officer in the United States Army:* 1981–1917.

Columbia, Maryland: University of Missouri Press, 1974.

Jones, Howard. *Mutiny on the Amistad: The Saga of a Slave Revolt and Its Impact on American Abolition, Law, and Diplomacy.* Oxford: Oxford University Press, 1988.

Lewis, David Levering. *W. E. B. Dubois: Biography of a Race.* New York: Henry Holt and Company, 1993.

Lewis, David Levering. "Parallels and Divergencies: Assimilationist Strategies of Afro- American and Jewish Elites from 1910 to the Early 1930s." *The Journal of American History 71*, December 1984.

Marable, Manning. "The Divided State of Black Leadership." *U.S. News and World Report*. July 18, 1994.

Melosi, Martin V. *Thomas A. Edison and the Modernization of America*. Edited by Oscar Handlin. New York: Harper Collins, 1990.

Merrill, Joey. "Mr. Chavis Goes to Washington: Reinventing the NAACP." *Diversity and Division: A Critical Journal of Race and Culture*, Fall 1993.

O'Neal, Bill. *Fighting Man of the Indian Wars*. Stillwater, Oklahoma: Barbed Wire Press, 1991.

Prouty, L. Fletcher. *The Secret Team: The C.I.A. and Its Allies in Control of the United States and the World*. Costa Mesa, California: Institute for Historical Review, 1973.

Robeson, Paul. *Here I Stand*. New York: Bantam Books, 1971.

Quarles, Benjamin. *The Negro in the Civil War*. Boston: Little, Brown, 1953.

Van Sectima, Ivan. *Blacks in Science*. New Brunswich, Connecticut: Transaction Books, 1986. West, Cornel. "The Dilemma of the Black Intellectual." *The Journal of Blacks in Higher Education*, Winter 199111994.

Woodson, Carter G. *The Miseducation of the Negro*. Trenton, New Jersey: Africa World Press, Inc. 1990.